EVANGELICAL PEACEMAKERS

Evangelical Peacemakers

Gospel Engagement in a War-Torn World

edited by

DAVID P. GUSHEE

CASCADE *Books* · Eugene, Oregon

EVANGELICAL PEACEMAKERS
Gospel Engagement in a War-Torn World

Cascade Books
An Imprint of Wipf and Stock Publishers
199 W. 8th Ave., Suite 3
Eugene, OR 97401

www.wipfandstock.com

ISBN 13: 978-1-62564-115-1

Cataloguing-in-Publication data:

Evangelical peacemakers : gospel engagement in a war-torn world / edited by David P. Gushee.

xiv + 136 pp. ; 23 cm. Includes bibliographical references.

ISBN 13: 978-1-62564-115-1

1. Evangelicalism—United States. 2. Peace—Religious aspects—Christianity. I. Gushee, David P. II. Title.

BT736.4 G75 2013.

Manufactured in the U.S.A.

To all who work for justice and peace in God's world

Contents

Contents

Contributors

SAMI AWAD is Executive Director of Holy Land Trust.

DAVID BEASLEY is former Republican Governor of South Carolina and a National Prayer Breakfast activist.

JOSEPH CUMMING is Director of the Reconciliation Program at the Yale Center for Faith and Culture at Yale Divinity School.

LISA R. GIBSON is Executive Director of the Peace and Prosperity Alliance and author of *Life in Death: A Journey from Terrorism to Triumph.*

DAVID P. GUSHEE is Distinguished University Professor of Christian Ethics and Director of the Center for Theology and Public Life at Mercer University, and the author/editor of fifteen books.

LISA SHARON HARPER is Director of Mobilizing at Sojourners and co-author of *Left, Right, and Christ: Evangelical Faith in Politics.*

MARK C. JOHNSON is Executive Director of the Fellowship of Reconciliation.

DOUGLAS M. JOHNSTON JR. is President of the International Center for Religion and Diplomacy and author of the award-winning *Religion, Terror, and Error: U.S. Foreign Policy and the Challenge of Spiritual Engagement.*

RICK LOVE is President of Peace Catalyst International and Associate Director of the World Evangelical Alliance Peace and Reconciliation Initiative.

ERIC PATTERSON is Dean of the Robertson School of Government at Regent University. He has previously worked at the U.S. State Department's Bureau of Political-Military Affairs and continues to serve as an officer in the Air National Guard.

Contributors

Bob Roberts Jr. is Senior Pastor of Northwood Church and author of numerous books, including *Glocalization: How Followers of Jesus Engage a Flat World.*

David W. Shenk is global consultant with Eastern Mennonite Missions and co-author of *A Muslim and a Christian in Dialogue.*

Glen Stassen is Lewis B. Smedes Professor of Christian Ethics at Fuller Seminary and author/editor of numerous books about just peacemaking.

Geoff Tunnicliffe is Chief Executive Officer/Secretary General, World Evangelical Alliance, serving and representing over 600 million evangelical Christians.

Jim Wallis is CEO of Sojourners and author of numerous books, including most recently *On God's Side.*

Preface and Acknowledgments

THIS VOLUME OFFERS THE collected and edited papers presented at the Evangelicals for Peace Summit on Christian Moral Responsibility in the Twenty-first Century, held at Georgetown University on September 14, 2012. The conference was organized primarily by Rick Love, president of Peace Catalyst International, a nonprofit whose purpose is "catalyzing peacemaking initiatives, for multi-dimensional reconciliation, in the way of Jesus." I extend my thanks both to Rick, for his creative work in pulling together the conference, and to Georgetown University, a Catholic school with a long history of hospitality to evangelicals and other people of faith from multiple traditions.

I was grateful to Rick to be invited to speak at this important conference, and then again grateful for the invitation to be the editor of the collected presentations. We were both quite happy when Rodney Clapp and the other leaders of Wipf and Stock agreed to publish the papers in this volume. Rodney Clapp is one of the most distinguished editors in Christian publishing and it is a personal joy to have had the chance to work with him again, now under the Cascade imprint.

The papers you are about to read can be said to have two foci.

The first four papers especially deal with longstanding, indeed agonizing, issues in the Christian theology and ethics of war, peace, and peacemaking. Pacifist, just war, and just peacemaking approaches are offered with skill and no little intensity.

- I (*David Gushee*) begin the book with a chapter suggesting that the U.S. has become a warfare state with a bloated national security apparatus and a pattern of excessive military engagements, but the obvious mistakes of the U.S. have made it difficult for American Christians to engage primal issues related to the moral legitimacy of possessing and sometimes deploying military force (chapter 1).

- *Lisa Sharon Harper* argues from the witness of Jesus Christ that redemptive love rather than violent conquest is God's way of exercising dominion on Earth. She goes on to describe and critique U.S. foreign policy after 9/11 (chapter 2).

- *Eric Patterson* presents a lengthy exposition and defense of just war theory, rooted especially in the writings of Augustine and Aquinas, as the most appropriate paradigm for Christian thinking about justice and security issues (chapter 3).

- *Glen Stassen* offers an exposition of just peacemaking and describes its ten practices as both faithful to Christ's teaching and effective in the real world (chapter 4).

In my concluding essay at the end of this collection I assess the strengths and weaknesses of these forays into the perennial debate about Christian ethical responsibility in relation to the tragic human problem of war.

The remainder of the papers primarily describe actual peacemaking efforts by evangelical churches, nongovernmental and parachurch organizations, and individuals:

- *Geoff Tunnicliffe* describes the peacemaking efforts of the World Evangelical Alliance, which he leads (chapter 5).

- *Mark Johnson* discusses the nearly one hundred years of peace witness of the Fellowship of Reconciliation, which he serves as president (chapter 6).

- *Joseph Cumming* of Yale University focuses on Christian peacemaking and witness in relation to the Muslim world (chapter 7).

- *Douglas Johnston* of the International Center for Religion and Diplomacy focuses on the need for U.S. foreign policy to take religion seriously both in general and especially in engaging predominantly Muslim nations (chapter 8).

- *David Shenk* describes peacemaking efforts of Mennonites and other Christians in some of the world's most intense conflict zones (chapter 9).

- *Lisa Gibson* describes the murder of her brother and hundreds of others by Libyan agents in the Lockerbie bombing of 1988, and her subsequent journey toward forgiveness, peacemaking, and service to the Libyan people (chapter 10).

- *Sami Awad*, a Palestinian Christian, discusses the peace-and justice-making witness of the Holy Land Trust organization that he leads (chapter 11).

- *Bob Roberts*, a megachurch pastor in Texas, describes his personal and congregational engagement serving Vietnam and Afghanistan in the name of Christ (chapter 12).

- *David Beasley*, former Republican governor of South Carolina, relates his efforts and that of his colleagues associated with the National Prayer Breakfast to bear loving witness to Jesus around the world (chapter 13).

- *Jim Wallis*, president of Sojourners, reviews almost fifty years of U.S. Christian peacemaking efforts (chapter 14).

- *Rick Love*, president of Peace Catalyst International, offers a six-point model for evangelical peacemaking (chapter 15).

For those who do not know evangelicals well, or who know us only by the hardline reputation of the 1980s–1990s Christian Right, these essays will come as a considerable surprise. They describe the gospel-motivated efforts of all different kinds of evangelicals to demonstrate the reconciling love of Jesus Christ in making peace in a war-torn world. I hasten to add what the authors themselves are too humble to say about themselves—many of these peacemaking efforts came (and continue) at considerable personal risk to the peacemakers themselves. You will read here of peacemaking efforts in dangerous lands like Iraq, Pakistan, and Afghanistan, and in not-especially-tourist destinations today like Egypt, Yemen, Indonesia, Lebanon, Libya, and Iran.

It helps to know that many of the contributors to this collection come out of missionary backgrounds, and many have served extensively in the Muslim world. What is visible here in this volume is not just a strikingly courageous evangelical peace- and justice-making, but also an emerging new approach to Christian missions and interfaith encounter. These are heart-and-soul evangelical Christians, but their understanding of what it means to be an evangelical is taking new and fascinating forms.

I can say all this without any kind of personal bragging, because my peacemaking work is far more academic than much of what is discussed here, and my international travel has been much safer. It has not taken me to visits with Hizbullah militants in Indonesia, to workshops with madrasa leaders in the radical areas of Pakistan, to encounters with Iranian ayatollahs in Tehran, or even into an audience with the late Muammar Gaddafi—all stories you will read here.

A major theme of these essays is Christian-Muslim encounter/dialogue/relationship-building/peacemaking. While after 9/11 a loud minority of evangelical and fundamentalist Christians were saying and writing all kinds of hateful things about Islam and about Muslims, these deeply devout evangelical Christians chose a different path. They chose human encounter in the name of, and in the Spirit of, Jesus Christ—not because they were less devout than the haters but because they were actually more devout, or at least, more faithful to Jesus. You owe it to yourself to read their stories here, for they are instructive for all Christians, and indeed all people of faith, in our deeply religious, deeply divided, deeply violent, world. These "Evangelical peacemakers" will give you hope—and perhaps even a model for how you might want to live out your own faith.

1 The U.S. Warfare State and Evangelical Peacemaking

DAVID P. GUSHEE

INTRODUCTION

I WILL TRY TO do three things in this opening chapter: offer an accurate critical assessment of contemporary United States foreign and military policy; offer an accurate critical assessment of contemporary evangelical engagement with U.S. foreign and military policy; and suggest some ways forward for evangelicals. I will state my claims primarily in the form of propositions, each of which could be and hopefully will be debated.

THE U.S. WARFARE STATE

The leaders of the federal government of the United States in the past twelve years have proven unable or unwilling to pass anything approaching a balanced budget. (Sometimes they can't pass any budget at all.) As annual deficits and cumulative debts mount, concern about our dramatic fiscal irresponsibility has moved to the center of political debate, with legitimate fears of a coming fiscal collapse as retiring baby boomer social security and health costs kick in. Zbigniew Brzezinski has recently argued that the ineffectiveness of our legislative process in addressing this basic task of governance contributes to a weakening respect for the United States abroad, itself an important foreign policy concern.[1]

And yet, amidst these fiscal problems, our $775 billion annual defense budget,[2] not to mention our tens of billions of dollars spent on intelligence and other national security expenses, is treated as sacrosanct. Budget-cutters, especially on the Republican side, do not train their sights on the defense budget as they seek to address our flood of red ink, but instead focus on dramatic cuts in the safety net for the poor.

According to former Reagan budget director David Stockman, our $775 billion defense budget is nearly twice as large in inflation-adjusted dollars as the defense budget of Dwight Eisenhower for 1961, during the Cold War.[3] Our fiscal year 2011 defense budget was five times greater than that of China, our nearest competition for this dubious honor; constituted over 40 percent of the world's entire military spending; and was larger than the cumulative budget of the next fourteen nations in the top fifteen.[4] All of this occurs at a time when our infrastructure is crumbling, our schools are sliding, and one-sixth of our population cannot find or has stopped looking for full-time work.[5]

The Republican David Stockman suggests that no plausible national defense goals today justify this level of defense spending. He rightly points out that "we have no advanced industrial state enemies" akin to the USSR of Cold War days. He argues that what in fact supports a budget of this size is an ideology of "neoconservative imperialism" and an attempt to function as a "global policeman" even after the world has "fired" us from this role.[6]

Andrew Bacevich argues in several important recent books that the direction of U.S. foreign and military policy is slipping from democratic control.[7] It is instead dominated by a cohort of active and retired military, intelligence, law enforcement, corporate, lobbyist, academic, and political elites whose power in Washington is sufficiently impressive as to foreclose serious reconsideration of what Bacevich calls the "Washington Rules." The elites enforcing these rules consistently drive us to policies of permanent

1. Brzezinski, *Strategic Vision*, 46–47.

2. Stockman, "Paul Ryan's Fairy-Tale Budget Plan."

3. Ibid.

4. "List of Countries by Military Expenditure."

5. Stiglitz, *Price of Inequality*, 1.

6. Stockman, "Paul Ryan's Fairy-Tale Budget Plan."

7. Bacevich, *Washington Rules*.

war, a staggeringly large global military presence, and regular global interventionism. This analysis stands in striking continuity with the warnings offered by President Eisenhower about the "military-industrial complex" fifty years ago.

U.S. foreign and military policy received scant attention in the 2012 presidential campaign, despite Governor Romney's efforts to position himself as more hawkish than President Obama, for example, in relation to Israel. But this had little effect, because President Obama has learned the lesson of prior Democratic presidents (and candidates) that no Democrat can afford to seem "soft on defense" or "weak" in foreign policy—that is, that no one dare break with the "Washington Rules." Thus only fringe politicians such as Ron Paul ever propose fundamental questions about the nature of our foreign and military policy.

While our taste for large boots-on-the-ground military interventions appears finally to have waned after the bloody and bankrupting off-budget wars in Iraq and Afghanistan, our special forces, covert, and technological intervention abroad—and the massive secret national security establishment that supports them—has heightened. Our nation has not had a serious debate about the centralization of presidential authority involved in this recent shift, including the legitimacy of presidential authority to order long-distance drone strikes—in countries that want such strikes, and in countries that don't want them.

The United States remains a nation traumatized by 9/11 and its terror attacks. We are easily manipulated into military and covert engagements in the name of post-9/11 national security.

One of the greatest tragedies of the last decade has been the extraordinary burden borne by the small cast of paid (e.g., "volunteer") soldiers who have been killed or traumatized by our recent wars. We honor them with sentimental displays at airports and ballparks, but seem to have no serious answer for mental health problems that now take twenty-five veteran's lives by suicide for every one soldier now dying on the battlefield.[8] And we will be paying their pensions and medical expenses for the next seventy years.

In a trenchant turn of phrase, David Stockman suggests that we have developed into a "warfare state"[9] whose military-spending excesses are one major factor contributing to economic decline and imminent fiscal emergency. I believe that David Stockman is correct.

8. Kristof, "War Wounds."
9. Stockman, "Paul Ryan's Fairy-Tale Budget Plan."

EVANGELICALS AND PEACE/WAR

The Christian, and not just evangelical, voice in U.S. foreign policy debates seems entirely marginalized, more so than at any time I have lived through or studied. There is no contemporary Christian leader, scholar, denomination, or movement whose views on U.S. foreign and military policies seems to matter to either party or its leaders.

Just war theory does not seem to be functioning in any significant or constructive way. In academia, its use seems to have become an empty intellectual exercise divorced from any persuasive power to guide either state policy or Christian practice. The outcome of just war theory reasoning seems tightly linked to the prior ideological or temperamental makeup of the just war theorist.

On the right, anti-Muslim and neo-Crusade thinking has resurfaced in both popular and academic circles, Christian and otherwise. This problem has obviously been exacerbated by the trauma of 9/11 and other acts of Islamist terrorism as well as the stresses of multiple U.S. military engagements in primarily Muslim lands.

Pacifism remains popular in elite academic and popular (progressive) circles. But it has little to offer to public discussion other than occasionally trenchant analyses of obvious excesses or wrongs in U.S. foreign and military policy. And most academic pacifism is untethered to actual Christian communities that practice either nonviolence or any other form of radical Christian discipleship.

Just peacemaking theory offers a profound strengthening of the last resort criterion of just war theory, as well as highlighting realistic conflict resolution possibilities through creative state and NGO diplomacy and grassroots citizen advocacy and action.[10] It is currently the most relevant of all existing Christian peacemaking theories/strategies but it would not be accurate to say that it has gained wide influence in U.S. foreign policy circles.

A longstanding coalition strategy within the center-left of evangelicalism has attempted to overcome differences between pacifists and just warriors by emphasizing areas of agreement and shared commitment to just peacemaking. This has protected friendships and produced strategic gains at times, but I wonder if it has weakened the concreteness, realism, and relevance of evangelical peacemaking efforts, and perhaps obscured the

10. Stassen, *Just Peacemaking*.

legitimate, principled differences between pacifists and those who believe Christians can sometimes support the use of force.

SOME WAYS FORWARD FOR EVANGELICAL PEACEMAKERS

We need to join the conversation about U.S. foreign and military policy. That includes studying U.S. foreign policy goals, our current military presence around the world, our alliance commitments, existing and planned weapons systems, and finally how all of that is reflected in the U.S. defense budget. We also need to become aware of the various political, civic, and economic forces that limit needed budget cuts in defense even when foreign policy and governmental leaders believe those cuts are actually needed. This is a formidable research agenda calling for the emergence of a new generation of ethics specialists in this area.

We need eventually to offer our own proposals, or join with those of others, for what kind of foreign policy, use of military force, and size and shape of defense budget that we could support. But this would require a willingness on our part to accept a legitimate national right of self-defense and use of lethal force under certain specified conditions. It would also involve consideration once again of the morality of maintaining military forces and weapons of sufficient scope to deter aggressors. In other words, we have to decide whether there is such a thing as "national security" that can find a place within a Christian approach, and if so, how a legitimate national security is best garnered and protected.

To do the above would involve accepting at least provisionally the stubborn existence of an entity called the nation-state, a world filled with an ever-shifting array of nation-states, and the internationally recognized right of those states to defend themselves. That is one price of admission to the conversation about how much defense to buy, for what purposes, etc. Currently in academia there is much critique of modernity, including the hegemony of the nation-state and its use of violence. This is really quite interesting, but meanwhile we live in a world with 190 nation-states, including our own, all of which are committed to defending themselves.

I suggest we need a swing back toward consideration of the difference between an ethic for Christian disciples and an ethic for the leaders of nations, states, political communities. The state is not the church. Even though I believe that the church qua church is called to be a nonviolent community, the state qua state cannot be a nonviolent community—though it can be called to exercise its security responsibilities as nonviolently as possible. The church can urge peace, we can pioneer peacemaking practices, and we can place ourselves at risk in order to create reconciliation opportunities between peoples and nations. But we must take seriously once again the classic conundrum that the statesperson, even the Christian statesperson, faces responsibilities involving the use of force in relation to protecting the people within his or her realm that others generally do not (cf. Rom 13:1–7). That is what U.S. military, intelligence, and diplomatic operatives do, and are supposed to be doing, even if their current mission needs dramatic trimming.

On a Tel Aviv Runway

I was sitting in an airplane on a runway in Tel Aviv this summer waiting for our plane to take off. We were at the point in the preparation for the flight when the attendants start telling passengers to power down their electronics. You know how it always takes several warnings. In this case, the young man next to me on the exit row kept defying these instructions. A flight attendant noticed and reminded him sternly to turn the phone off and put it away. As we were taxiing out to the runway he slipped the phone out of his pocket and started messing with it again. This time the flight attendant got out of her seat, stood right over the man, and officially threatened him with a $10,000 fine if the phone was not shut off and put away. He complained about how he was finishing a conversation with the small son he was leaving back in Israel. The attendant was unmoved. Finally he put the phone away.

So what did I witness? I witnessed the use of coercive power against a person whose behavior violated the law and was believed to pose a threat to the safety of others. The power of the state, through the designated airline authority, was imposed by coercion on this passenger against his will on behalf of everyone else.

As I pondered the power of the state to take $10,000 away from my seatmate for using his cellphone, I thought of other far more serious scenarios. What if this man had waited thirty minutes and instead of using a cellphone unlawfully had rushed to the emergency exit right in front of us and tried to wrestle it open? Or what if he had tried to set off a bomb?

There is something about the utter vulnerability of an airplane at 30,000 feet—especially after 9/11—that reminds us that there really is such a thing as a lethal threat against innocent people, and that the state really does have a responsibility to deter, prevent, and punish such threats. Indeed, the airplane scenario reminded me that it is actually the responsibility of any able-bodied person on an airplane to participate in that security project, as has occurred several times in recent years. I reflected that if faced with the necessity of preventing someone from killing everyone on an airplane, it would be my moral obligation to do what I could to defend innocent life, using the least violent means necessary, of course. In Christian terms, to do so would be an aspect of the love of neighbor commanded by Jesus, not a defiance of my Lord. Thinking about my recalcitrant seatmate helped me reconnect the use of force to the obligation to love my neighbor, which takes just war theory back to its roots.[11]

I want to test a hypothesis with you: what if the thinking of U.S. center-left Christians, including evangelicals, has been somewhat misshaped by the increasingly obvious wrongs of U.S. foreign and military policy for the last sixty-five years, including the first use of nuclear weapons in 1945, the insane nuclear arms race with its Mutual Assured Destruction madness, the deployment and planned use of nuclear weapons in various theaters of war, the foolish conventional-but-devastating wars in Vietnam, Iraq, and elsewhere, and the bloating of our military budget as outlined earlier? What if because U.S. foreign and military policy has been potentially lethal to the planet, as well as bankrupting, unwise, and neo-imperialistic, this reality has obscured for us historic issues in Christian thinking about war that go back at least as far as Ambrose? What if we simply haven't had to deal with the most basic and ancient questions about whether or how peoples on this planet legitimately defend their lives against aggressors, because until the recent domestic terror attacks this was not the most urgent question when thoughtful Christians engaged U.S. foreign policy?

These are at least the questions raised for me as I consider the nexus between the U.S. warfare state and evangelical peacemaking.

---

11. Bell, *Just War as Christian Discipleship*.

2 War, Terror, and Peace

LISA SHARON HARPER

> "Blessed are the meek, for they will inherit the earth."
>
> —MATTHEW 5:5

> "Put your sword back into its place;
> for all who take the sword will perish by the sword."
>
> —MATTHEW 26:52

IT WAS 8:30 AM in Los Angeles. My apartment mate, Donna, banged on my door, ran into my room, and woke me up out of a deep sleep yelling: "The World Trade Center is gone and America is at war!"

In the aftermath of the horror—after people fell from the sky, black clouds of dust filled with steel, concrete and flesh pushed screaming New Yorkers out of downtown Manhattan and across the iconic Brooklyn Bridge, one-fifth of the Pentagon was decimated by an airplane strike and another plane went down over Shanksville, Pennsylvania—after it all America went on lock-down. Airports across the country shut down. No one could get into or out of the United States. And no one knew when or where or if there would be another attack.

Nearly 3,000 people died on September 11, 2001, including the nineteen hijackers who carried out the attacks.

That day was a hinge point in the history, the trajectory, and the very culture of the United States of America—9/11 changed everything.

Thomas Hammarberg, Commissioner for Human Rights at the Council of Europe, has said, "The problem is not whether or not we will react to terrorists, but how?"[1]

How does Jesus answer terror?

The author of the apocryphal Fourth Book of Ezra describes the empire of Rome as a terrorist state, the last of four occupying beasts:

> You, the fourth that has come, have conquered all the beasts that have gone before; and you have sway over the world with much terror, and over all the earth with grievous oppression; and for so long you have dwelt on the earth with deceit. And you have judged the earth, but not with truth; for you have afflicted the meek and injured the peaceable; you have hated those who tell the truth, and have loved liars; you have destroyed the dwellings of those who brought forth fruit, and have laid low the walls of those who did you no harm.[2]

In 63 BC Pompey conquered Judea and claimed it as a client kingdom of Rome. In 6 AD Augustus Caesar made Judea a Roman province. The occupying Roman beast was on the march. In the days when Jesus walked the earth, the Zealots bore arms to free the Jews of their Roman occupiers. They were considered terrorists by the Roman state. In *The War on Terrorism and the Terror of God*, Lee Griffith explains that in precisely this context "Jesus admonished his followers to turn the other cheek, to love enemies, and to do good to persecutors."[3]

In the chapter on "War and Terror" in my book *Left, Right, and Christ: Evangelical Faith in Politics*, which serves as the basis of these reflections, I ask the reader to imagine being Simon the Zealot (the terrorist) "who believes in the use of violence to fight violence and the poverty caused by Israel's Roman occupation. Jesus has just chosen him to be his follower . . ."[4] Can you see it? Now see Jesus. He sits Simon down with the other eleven disciples and says:

> Blessed are the poor in spirit, for theirs is the kingdom of heaven.
> Blessed are those who mourn, for they will be comforted. Blessed

---

1. Quoted by Gerald Staberock, Skype interview with author, February 3, 2011.
2. Quoted in Griffith, *The War on Terrorism and the Terror of God*, 21.
3. Ibid., 23.
4. Harper and Innes, *Left, Right, and Christ*, 186.

are the meek, for they will inherit the earth. Blessed are those who hunger and thirst for justice, for they will be filled. Blessed are the merciful, for they will receive mercy. Blessed are the peacemakers, for they will be called children of God. Blessed are those who are persecuted for justice's sake, for theirs is the kingdom of heaven. Blessed are you when people revile you and persecute you and utter all kinds of evil against you falsely on my account. Rejoice and be glad, for your reward is great in heaven, for in the same way they persecuted the prophets who were before you. (Matthew 5:3–12, NRSV, adapted by author)

Griffith explains, "The admonitions of the Sermon on the Mount were understood as literal ethical guidance."[5] Jesus served as the great rabbi and demonstrated what it looks like to live according to his own ethical teachings when he himself was faced with the Roman Empire's primary instrument of terror—the cross.

Judas betrayed Jesus with a kiss in the garden of Gethsemane. A detachment of Roman soldiers along with police from the chief priests and Pharisees moved to seize Jesus. Just then, in a bold act of defiance, Peter took out his sword and sliced off the right ear of a man named Malchus, a slave of one of the chief priests. Jesus commanded, "Put your sword back into its place; for all who take the sword will perish by the sword." And he touched the slave's ear and it was healed (Matt 26:52, Luke 22:51, John 18:1–11).

Then, as I explain in *Left, Right, and Christ*, "Jesus stared into the faces of people who considered him their enemy and he turned his other cheek. Jesus allowed himself to be whipped. He allowed spikes to be driven into his wrists and ankles. He allowed a terrorist state to use his death as a horrifying warning to any who dare follow him from this point on."[6] Allegiance to Jesus would be a direct challenge to the deity of Caesar and to the ultimate authority of occupying Rome. Follow Jesus and die.

Why didn't Jesus fight? The people had been waiting for a Messiah to overthrow Caesar by force. If it was going to happen, it had to happen in that very moment. Why did Jesus rebuke Peter? And further, why did Jesus heal the slave's ear? Why did he walk the path of silence and nonviolent resistance with Pilate rather than lashing out or arguing his case? (Matt 27:11–14). And why did Jesus turn the other cheek? Why did he exercise meekness, which means disciplined power, while staring terror in the face?

5. Griffith, *The War on Terrorism and the Terror of God*, 23.

6. Harper and Innes, *Left, Right, and Christ*, 187.

I believe it was because in the faces of the chief priests, and their slaves, and the Roman soldiers, and Caesar himself, Jesus saw the image of God. I ask, "How could Jesus strike down the image of God? He came to redeem and restore the image of God on earth, to set the slaves, and the soldiers, and the priests free from the violent reign of men. He came that Caesar himself might be brought back to life by the dominion of God."[7] From the picture of creation in Genesis 1 and 2 to the establishment of Israel in Exodus, Deuteronomy, Leviticus, and Numbers to the cries of the prophets Isaiah, Jeremiah, Micah, and Ezekiel, scripture paints a picture of God's kind of dominion. It is characterized by disciplined power, servant leadership, truth-telling, just dealing, reconciliation and reparation, and above all else love. I believe Jesus did not fight because Jesus believed in redemption.

Considering the effect of ethical dualism on the paradigms we develop in times of conflict, Griffith reflects, "Conquest comes through the infliction of suffering. Redemption comes through the Suffering Servant."[8] My co-author in *Left, Right, and Christ*, D. C. Innes, states: "God authorizes the sword, because there are cruel beasts at the city gates who [sic] will not depart unless they are either destroyed or credibly threatened with destruction."[9] This is not my worldview. I and my nation are not inherently good and those who might come against me or my nation are not automatically cast as evil. Rather, the entire world and all relationships in it suffer under the repercussions of the fall (Gen 3).

We are all fallen. We all suffer the consequences of the choices we all make to exercise a human kind of dominion rather than God's kind of dominion. We suffer the consequences of our bids to secure our kind of peace—the kind of peace that comes at the expense of the peace of others. Griffith illuminates the key distinction between my paradigm and that of my co-author: "These are sharply contrasting views of the world: a world filled with evil in need of conquest, or a suffering creation groaning for redemption."[10]

Gerald Staberock, the deputy secretary general of the World Organization against Torture in Switzerland, explains the effect of the ethical dualism embedded in the paradigm of war. "The war paradigm works on

7. Ibid., 185.

8. Griffith, *The War on Terrorism and the Terror of God*, 76.

9. Harper and Innes, *Left, Right, and Christ*, 176.

10. Griffith, *The War on Terrorism and the Terror of God*, 76.

an 'us vs. them' framework . . . If you speak in the terms of war you only have friends and enemies."[11]

The United States is a nation founded on core values: the rights of the individual, the protection of the rights of minorities, the rule of law, free and fair elections, and due process all make up the pillars of our democracy. In a legal paradigm, Staberock explained, you have the law, the courts, time-tested processes, and with these you protect your values. In a war paradigm all bets are off. Individual liberties are often severely limited or sacrificed, minorities are vulnerable to scapegoating, and the rule of law is limited because laws change or are suspended in wartime. For example, killing is forbidden in all circumstances in a legal paradigm. In a war paradigm it is not only excusable, but states are expected to kill "the enemy."

Consider the results of President George W. Bush's "global war on terror." First, according to international law, wars can only be declared against nation-states, not against individual actors or networks. The declaration unleashed a new norm with no end in sight within American life; the norm of dehumanization and disregard for the rule of law. The era has no end because how can one name the endpoint of a "global war on terror"? Bush's use of the war paradigm led to the adoption of dehumanizing tactics like torture and the detention of U.S. citizens and residents at Guantanamo Bay. A national commission recently confirmed that the United States did, in fact, break domestic and international law with the use of torture tactics during the Iraq war.[12]

The U.S. answered the horror of 9/11 with the paradigm of war; conquest not redemption, "us vs. them" and "friends vs. enemies," not law. One might argue that the terrorists won on 9/11. Terror laid hold of the American soul and, under the guise of strength, America weakened its grip on its fundamental values: due process, the rule of law, protection of the rights of minorities, and the rights of individuals. Also as a result, the pervasive presence of the military and the mechanisms of war have become normative in everyday American life.

On September 10, 2001 military personnel were not a regular part of the landscape of every airport and train station. At airports, friends could meet flyers at their flight gate. On September 10, 2001 it had been more than twenty-five years since America's last major war and the most

11. Staberock, interview with the author.

12. Scott Shane, "U.S. Engages in Torture After 9/11; Review Concludes," *New York Times*, April 16, 2013.

popular television shows were shows like *Sex in the City, ER*, and *Moesha and Friends.* After September 11th, a constant military presence and images of violence permeated our culture. Everyday entertainment became *24, CSI, Breaking Bad, The Wire*, and a plethora of military video games. According to a recent report by MotherJones.com, there were thirty-three mass shootings from 1982 to 2002 (twenty years). There have been almost as many mass shootings (twenty-nine) in almost half that time since 9/11 (twelve years).[13]

President Obama inherited the legal chaos created by former President Bush's war paradigm and tolerance of torture and a culture where violence has become normative. In the first years of his presidency, he systematically strengthened our cooperation with and accountability to the United Nations and international and human rights law bodies. Yet, President Obama has a long way to go to live up to his stated commitment to the rule of law and due process. To reconcile his promises with his policies he must close the Guantanamo Bay prison.

As I stated in *Left, Right, and Christ*: "War is not inevitable. We have choices. We can choose the licentiousness of war and terror or the disciplined power of law and meek redemption of broken international relationships. War does not ultimately save us from evil-doers; it transforms the principled into perpetrators. We must do everything within our power to find another way."[14]

13. Follman, Aronsen, and Pan, "U.S. Mass Shootings, 1982–2012."
14. Harper and Innes, *Left, Right, and Christ*, 194.

3 Just War Theory

Christian Teaching on Justice and Security

Eric Patterson

IN *MONTY PYTHON AND The Holy Grail* King Arthur fights the Black Knight who opposes anyone who wants to cross a certain bridge. Arthur had just seen the Black Knight defeat another challenger, and offers him a seat at Camelot. But, the Black Knight attacks Arthur. In this legendary film scene, Arthur cuts off the Black Knight's appendages one by one in the course of battle, while the Black Knight famously replies, "Just a flesh wound . . . come back you pansy, I'll bite your legs off!"

Much could be said about the Black Knight as a representative of Al Qaeda, or Hitler, or many other regimes: rabid individuals and leaders who will stop at nothing in their quest to steal, kill, and destroy. Leaving the enemy aside, however, what does Arthur represent in this scene? Arthur symbolizes, beyond the hilarity, the rule of law and the imperatives of political order. If Arthur did not deal with the Black Knight, who would? If the king did not impose order in his realm, who would? What would happen to the next peasant who needed to use that bridge for commerce? If Arthur, if the state, did not deal with the situation, how would justice be promoted? Would the King of the Britons have shown more love of neighbor by ignoring the Black Knight ("he is not my problem") or by promoting the rule of law?

The Christian just war tradition provides answers to these questions and more. As this volume is dedicated to evangelical thought on issues of security and peace, it would be best if evangelicals began with an attitude of humility by examining Christian teaching over the past 1,800 years on the subjects of war, violence, politics, security, and peace. Mainstream Christian thought, from Ambrose and Augustine in the Roman era to Paul Ramsey in the late twentieth century, all took the just war perspective as the normal and normative position for Christians when considering these issues. This chapter provides a brief overview of the just war tradition with examples of two of its most important Christian thinkers, and then elucidates some of the key presuppositions of the tradition that make it superior to other schools of thought on these issues.

WHAT IS JUST WAR THEORY?

The just war tradition is a body of principles derived from theory and practice over the past two millennia.[1] This list by well-known just war thinker and historian James Turner Johnson is a classic, basic exposition of those principles taken directly from his book *Morality and Contemporary Warfare*.[2]

The jus ad bellum: Criteria defining the right resort to force

- *Just Cause*: The protection and preservation of value (e.g., defense of the innocent against armed attack, retaking of persons, property or other values wrongly taken, punishment of evil).

- *Right Authority*: The person or body authorizing the use of force must be the duly authorized representative of a sovereign political entity. The authorization to use force implies the ability to control and cease that use: that is, a well-constituted and efficient chain of command.

- *Right Intention*: The intent must be in accord with the just cause and not territorial aggrandizement, intimidation, or coercion.

- *Proportionality of Ends*: The overall good achieved by the use of force must be greater than the harm done. The levels and means of using force must be appropriate to the just ends sought.

---

1. See Johnson, *Morality and Contemporary Warfare*; Walzer, *Just and Unjust Wars*; Stephenson, *Christian Love and Just War*; Patterson, *Just War Thinking*; Elshtain, *Just War Against Terror*; Biggar, *Burying the Past*; Weigel, *Tranquillitas Ordinis*.

2. Johnson, *Morality and Contemporary Warfare*, 28–29.

- *Last Resort*: Determination at the time of the decision to employ force that no other means will achieve the justified ends sought. Interacts with other *jus ad bellum* criteria to determine level, type, and duration of force employed.

- *Reasonable Hope of Success*: Prudential calculation of the likelihood that the means used will bring the justified ends sought. Interacts with other jus ad bellum criteria to determine level, type, and duration of force employed.

- *The Aim of Peace*: Establishment of international stability, security, and peaceful interaction. May include nation building, disarmament, and other measure to promote peace.

The jus in bello: Criteria defining the employment of force

- *Proportionality of Means*: Means causing gratuitous or otherwise unnecessary harm are to be avoided. Prohibition of torture, means *mala in se*.

- *Noncombatant Protection/Immunity*: Definition of non-combatancy, avoidance of direct, intentional harm to noncombatants, efforts to protect them.

Excellent volumes have been written on the history of just war theory, making a full presentation here redundant,[3] although it is noteworthy that a fresh volume by Professor J. Darryl Charles and former Navy chaplain Timothy Demy answers hundreds of questions—citing dozens of historical Christian texts—about the ethics of war from a Christian perspective.[4] In this volume they do look carefully at the earliest extant Christian writers, such as Polycarp, Origen, Tertullian, and Eusebius on questions of government and the military. These thinkers have been wrongly identified as "pacifists," but as Charles and Demy demonstrate, the early Christian writers were much more concerned with the pagan religious duties that Roman magistrates and soldiers had to perform as part of their everyday jobs, including kneeling to idols, acknowledging the deity of the emperor, participating in various sacral feasts and ceremonies, and the like. The

3. Russell, *The Just War in the Middle Ages*; Johnson, *The Just War Tradition and the Restraint of War*.

4. Charles and Demy, *War, Peace, and Christianity*.

second- and third-century church was deeply concerned about these activities as idol worship rather than questioning the efficacy of just magistrates, police, and security personnel.

Charles and Demy are among those who remind us that Christianity has two millennia of teaching on government and the use of force, and modern evangelicals should start their deliberations with modest and intent study on what the great churchmen of the past have to say on these issues. The most important of such authors, one cited as an authority by not only Catholic political theorists and churchmen but also by Luther and Calvin as authoritative, is Augustine, Bishop of Hippo.

Augustine (354–430 AD) traveled across the Roman world and saw the glories and perversions of imperial Rome. As a Christian observing both the Pax Romana and the cruelties of the arena, Augustine pondered the conditions for when it was just to employ violence in political life. Augustine's formulation of the just use of force relied heavily on the notion of *caritas*, or charity: "love your neighbor as yourself." In domestic society as well as international life, how does one go about loving one's neighbor? Augustine argued that within society adherence to the rule of law, including punishment of lawbreakers, was a way of loving one's neighbors. When one loves one's neighbors one refrains from harming them and supports the authorities in their efforts to provide security to the citizenry. Moreover, Augustine noted, *caritas* means protecting one's neighbor when he or she is attacked, even if one is forced to employ violence to protect that individual. Augustine used Romans 13:1–5 to argue that sovereign authorities have a responsibility to order and to justice, including the use of the sword:

> Let every soul be subject unto the higher powers. For there is no power but of God: the powers that be are ordained of God. Whosoever therefore resists the power, resists the ordinance of God: and they that resist shall receive to themselves damnation. For rulers are not a terror to good works, but to evil. Wilt thou then not be afraid of the power? Do that which is good, and thou shalt have praise of the same. For he [the government official] is the minister of God to thee for good. But if thou do that which is evil, be afraid. For he beareth not the sword in vain: for he is the minister of God, a revenger to execute wrath upon him that doeth evil. Wherefore ye must needs be subject, not only for wrath, but also for conscience sake (KJV).

Augustine suggested that this is also true with regards to foreign threats: loving our neighbor can mean self-defense of the polity. Likewise, loving our foreign neighbors may mean using force to punish evildoers or right a wrong. He writes, "True religion looks upon as peaceful those wars that are waged not for motives of aggrandizement, or cruelty, but with the object of securing peace, of punishing evil-doers, and of uplifting the good."[5]

In addition to *caritas*, Augustine's writings suggest a second reason for *jus ad bellum*: order. Augustine consistently privileged political order over disorder. The Augustinian conception of the universe is one in which God is the ultimate Creator, Judge, Arbiter, and End. Although God allows sin and imperfection in this world, he nonetheless sustains the universe with a divine order. This order is mirrored in society by the political order with its laws and hierarchy. Augustine argued that although the City of Man is a poor reflection of the City of God, nonetheless it is the political principle of temporal order—based on the concept of justice—that most approximates the eternal order.[6] During his lifetime Augustine witnessed the alternative: the looting of Rome and ultimately the sacking of his home in North Africa in the final days of his life. Augustine's fear of political disorder was more than a distaste for regime change, it was dread of losing civic order with all of its attendant moral duties and opportunities.

Today, many Christians want to focus on the law of love but neglect Augustine's presupposition that political order is the foundation for society.[7] Augustine's argument is that the state has a responsibility for both domestic and international security—a responsibility that it must uphold, even if the state dirties its hands in the process of securing the realm.

Augustine's intellectual heir was Thomas Aquinas (1225–1274), who argued that a war was just when it met three requirements: sovereign authority, just cause, and right intent. It is noteworthy that Aquinas began not with just cause or right intent, but with *sovereign authority*:

> In order for a war to be just, three things are necessary. First, the authority of the sovereign by whose command the war is to be waged. For it is not the business of a private individual to declare war . . . And as the care of the common weal is committed to those who are in authority, it is their business to watch over the common weal of the city, kingdom or province subject to them. And just as it is lawful for them to have recourse to the sword in defending that common weal against internal disturbances, when they

---

5. Quoted in Aquinas, *Summa Theologica*, Part II, II, Question 40.

6. Epp, "Augustinian Moment."

7. Patterson, *Christian Realists*, ch. 1.

punish evil-doers . . . so too, it is their business to have recourse to the sword of war in defending the common weal against external enemies.[8]

Aquinas saw most violence as criminal and lawless. The fundamental purpose of the state was to provide a counterpoise to lawlessness.

Aquinas also argued that states should be concerned with *just cause*. He writes: "Secondly, a just cause is required, namely that those who are attacked, should be attacked because they deserve it on account of some fault." He quotes Augustine: "Wherefore Augustine says: 'A just war is wont to be described as one that avenges wrongs, when a nation or state has to be punished, for refusing to make amends for the wrongs inflicted by its subjects, or to restore what it has seized unjustly.'"[9] Aquinas's conception of just cause is richer than the contemporary debate on self-defense because it includes punishing wrongdoing and restitution of some sort to victims. Indeed, it seems that Aquinas's just cause would support the use of force to curb aggressive non-state actors, protect individual human life via humanitarian intervention, and punish rogue regimes that disrupt the international status quo.

Finally, Aquinas said that the just resort to force required *just intent*. Scholars and churchmen alike have long pointed out the dilemmas of ascertaining right intent. For the average soldier, the medievals solved this problem by providing absolution to their troops before battle and sometimes providing it again after the battle for the survivors. This did not completely solve the problem of rage and bloodlust on the battlefield, but sought a spiritual solution to a very human dynamic.

However, this says little about the sovereign's motivation. Contemporary politics makes the situation even more complex because most state decisions are not made by a sovereign individual such as a king or empress. Western governments are pluralistic, representing multiple voices and acting based on a complicated set of interests and ideals. However, Aquinas's focus on right intent did not necessarily call for agonizing over one's ethical motivations. He writes, "Thirdly, it is necessary that the belligerents should have a rightful intention, so that they intend the advancement of good, or the avoidance of evil." In other words, Aquinas's idea of right intent is that states should seek to advance the security of their people and avoid wars based only on greed or vengeance. Aquinas again cites Augustine:

8. Aquinas, *Summa Theologica*, Part II, II, Question 40.

9. Ibid.

"Hence Augustine says: 'The passion for inflicting harm, the cruel thirst for vengeance, an unpacific and relentless spirit, the fever of revolt, the lust of power, and such like things, all these are rightly condemned in war.'"[10] Aquinas would likely agree that in contemporary international politics, the right intent of states is to seek their own security and then promote human life around the world.

It is beyond the scope of this essay to deal with all of the great Christian thinkers and their views on the ethics of war, but nearly every question conceivable about the ethics of armed conflict and the responsibilities of the individual and the state can be found therein with a little study: Aquinas on self-defense against the Turks, Vitoria and Suarez criticizing Spanish treatment of native people in the New World, Hugo Grotius articulating an international law outside of ecclesiastical mandates, Martin Luther and John Calvin emphasizing the importance of a robust state and the ethics of self-defense, and others in our own time, most notably Paul Ramsey on just war in the nuclear age and Jean Bethke Elshtain's recent work on gross human rights violations and the possibilities of justice and forgiveness. Even that most beloved of all twentieth century Protestant apologists, C. S. Lewis, briefly refuted pacifism as irresponsible: "Does anyone suppose that our Lord's hearers understood him to mean that if a homicidal maniac, attempting to murder a third party, tried to knock me out of the way, I must step aside and let him get his victim?"[11] All of this work is the heritage of modern Christians, and is worthy of our reference.

CONSIDERATIONS AND ASSUMPTIONS FOR TODAY

With this in mind, it is best to go back to first principles and consider some of the underlying assumptions of the tradition, in part so that we can meet the arguments of both the holy warriors (e.g., among violent Islamists) as well as the radical (or naive) pacifists in evangelical churches. Most importantly, the just war tradition stems from the notion of neighbor-love. Consequently, how do political authorities, how do law enforcement officials, how do soldiers, how do statesmen, how do leaders and public servants employ neighbor-love in collective situations? Beyond how I (the individual) love my immediate neighbor (the individual), how do political leaders put neighbor-love into practice? Theologian Paul Ramsey recognized the

10. Ibid.

11. Lewis, "Why I Am Not a Pacifist," 86.

difference between individual Christians and the duties of political leaders: "Love, which by its nature would be non-resistant where only the agent's own rights and the perhaps unjust claims of a single neighbor are involved, may change its action to resistance by the most effective possible means, judicial or military, violent or non-violent, when the needs of more than one neighbor come into view."[12]

Consequently, how should the President of the United States demonstrate love for the American polity and its allies? How does one work out an ethic of neighbor-love when one's nation is attacked, such as at Pearl Harbor? Or when an ally is swallowed up by a dictator, like the Sudetenland by Hitler or Kuwait in 1990–1991? How should we fulfill our solemn covenants, like the Genocide Convention (a legally-binding treaty), when genocide occurs in the Balkans or Africa? How do you/we/us put this into practice? Fortunately, we have a longstanding framework called the just war tradition that deals with this.

As C. S. Lewis suggests, political leaders employing force is not evil in and of itself: ". . . it harmonizes better with St. John [the] Baptist's words to the soldier and with the fact that one of the few persons whom Our Lord praised without reservation was a Roman centurion. It also allows me to suppose that the New Testament is consistent with itself. St. Paul approves of the magistrate's use of the sword (Romans 13:4) and so does St. Peter (1 Peter 2:14)."[13] Political leaders fulfilling their obligations to protect, prevent, and punish does not result in them necessarily incurring morally "dirty hands." In fact, employing force can be a virtuous act. A policeman is not morally tainted by doing his job in a professional manner. Force can be employed by that policeman in a way that is moral, and the same holds true for political leaders who employ the military instrument, and for the soldiers who do so.

The just war tradition emphasizes intentions, and in particular the differences between righteous indignation and hatred as well as justice versus revenge. There really is a difference between right intent, which is defined in terms of security, and justice, and retribution, which are all biblical principles, and an intention of revenge. Revenge is that insatiable desire to crush the other side. Revenge goes beyond justice to hatred and unrestrained harm. As C. S. Lewis writes, "We may [in wartime] kill if necessary, but we must never hate and enjoy hating. We may punish if necessary, but

---

12. Ramsey, *Basic Christian Ethics*, 165.

13. Lewis, "Why I Am Not A Pacifist," 87.

we must not enjoy it. In other words, something inside of us, the feeling of resentment, the feeling that wants to get one's own back, must be simply killed. . . . It is hard work, but the attempt is not impossible."[14]

Just war thinking also distinguishes between political authorities employing force and private citizens taking matters into their own hands. Anglican theological Oliver O'Donovan writes, "It is the essential structure of government to harness representative status and power to the service of the judgment and the law. That structure is the provision of common grace, and without it our best efforts at making peace are doomed to be swept away."[15] In other words, at times political authorities must deploy force and it is not immoral for them to do so. The just war tradition knows that there is a distinction between violence and the use of force by legitimate authorities. The difference is that the use by proper authorities is, in theory, proportional and limited in contrast to the unrestrained use of force by non-governmental actors acting outside of the law.

Another presupposition, of particular import to many evangelicals, comes from Protestant theology about vocations: there are different callings and vocations in Christendom. Some Christians are called to be pastors, some are called to be apostles, and some are called to be teachers. Most Protestant traditions also believe that there are people who are called to be nurses, and doctors, and other vocations of help, and likewise that there will be some who are called to serve in government. Some individuals are called to be political leaders. Thus, promoting public order by serving in the military, law enforcement, emergency services, or public office are vocations in which one can be virtuous in pursuing their calling. Martin Luther recognized this solemn obligation: "If the ruler does not fulfill the duties of his office by punishing some and protecting others, he commits as great a sin before God as when someone who has not been given the sword commits murder."[16]

Some erroneously believe that just war thinking fundamentally is incompatible with religion-inspired peacemaking. This is simply not true. As Scott Appleby argues in his superb book *The Ambivalence of the Sacred*, and as I have argued elsewhere, there is a role for peacemaking and peace-building by religious individuals. In general, the right time for these efforts is a) on the front end of conflict in preventative action, and b) on the back

---

14. Lewis, *Mere Christianity*, 109.

15. O'Donovan, *The Just War Revisited*, 32.

16. Tappert, ed., *Selected Writings of Martin Luther, 1529-1546*, 353.

end in post-conflict humanitarian aid and reconciliation.[17] But these vocations do not erase the need for other people to guide policy, and for some whose vocations are to serve in public service and thereby protect the weak.

There is a frontier in just war thinking where there is contemporary intellectual ferment: it is the ethics of late- and post-conflict, *jus post bellum*. Traditional just war theory said little formally about *jus post bellum* as a distinct category within the just war tradition. The reason for this lacuna is not because the just war tradition did not care about war's end. It is because just war theory in its Christian application is just a narrow sliver of the larger philosophical milieu of Christendom. More specifically, just war theory answers just one small set of questions about the role of the Christian and Christianity in society that major Christian works, like Augustine's *City of God*, Aquinas's *Summae Theologica*, or even Lewis's *Mere Christianity*, address. All of these have a few things to say about war, but they have much more to say about morality, justice, politics, and society: all of which help us answer the question, "How should wars end?" However, there is emerging a vibrant literature on this topic, led by authors such as Orend, Patterson, and others.[18]

Conclusion

This chapter argues that the Christian just war tradition provides substantive direction for the evangelical community to wrestle with issues of ethics and the use of force. There is plenty in the Christian tradition to remind us that political and security vocations are not evil vocations, beginning with the fact that Jesus, John the Baptist, Paul, and other New Testament figures did not tell soldiers to lay down their weapons or political authorities to leave their posts. Moreover, Paul's letter to the Romans (chapter 13) and Peter's second epistle emphasize the role of political authorities in providing for the public good, in particular by wielding the sword. In the twentieth century, Protestant thinkers like Reinhold Niebuhr, Dietrich Bonhoeffer, C. S. Lewis, and Paul Ramsey demonstrated the moral courage to take a stand against the evils of violent Nazism and Communism, while at the same time often criticizing the lesser injustices inherent in their own societies. More recently, Christian thinkers from a variety of traditions, including

17. Appleby, *Ambivalence of the Sacred*; Patterson, *Politics in a Religious World*.

18. Orend, "Justice After War"; Orend, *Morality of War*, 160–89. Also Patterson, *Ending Wars Well*, and Patterson, ed., *Ethics Beyond War's End*.

George Weigel, Jean Bethke Elshtain, J. Darryl Charles, Oliver O'Donovan, and others have applied the Christian just war tradition to the issues of mass trauma, political reconciliation in the aftermath of war, terrorism, and contemporary conflict.

In the end, just war thinking is about "neighbor-love" in a collective sense: how can we (as a polity) love our neighbors? How can we promote a security Golden Rule: to work toward the kind of peace and security that we want our own family to enjoy, on a regional and global scale? How can we "love our neighbor(s) as ourselves"? The best way to operationalize neighbor-love in the real world of limits, fallenness, and evil is by employing the moral reasoning provided by just war theory.

4 Learn and Teach the Practices that Make for Peace

GLEN STASSEN

I IMAGINE MOST OF us resonate strongly with David Gushee's challenge about military spending and the powerful military-industrial and ideological complex. I surely do.

Today the military budget is approximately $800 billion, including the cost of two wars that were initiated by the U.S. government in Afghanistan and Iraq. And with the Great Recession that began in 2008 and is only slowly lifting as I write in 2012, the party under whose policies the Great Recession began is now clamoring against the deficit but saying taxes cannot be raised—let alone restored to Clinton levels that balanced the budget—and the military budget must be increased. Yet the military budget is now so large it is the majority of the discretionary part of the budget that could be cut. Mathematically, to reduce the deficit without raising taxes while increasing the military budget would require cutting many teachers, unemployment payments, job stimulus programs, Pell Grants and college loans, Food Stamps and programs for the poor, and aid to hungry nations. And none of this would come close to plugging the hole in the budget.

Furthermore, military spending produces far fewer jobs than education, environmental technology, and rebuilding bridges, because one soldier in Afghanistan costs about $1 million per year. Even more if you add the enormous cost of rehabilitating the wounded and those with PTSD, and the loss of those who commit suicide. One teacher or construction worker costs only about $50,000 per year. Therefore, $1 million pays for the job for one soldier in Afghanistan, or pays for jobs for about twenty teachers or construction workers. Outside Afghanistan, military spending produces one-third as many jobs as spending for education or rebuilding infrastructure (see www.nationalpriorities.org).

PACIFISM AND JUST WAR ALONE ARE NOT EMPOWERING

But as David Gushee's essay suggests, to focus on pacifism or just war has proven to be disempowering. Just to say no to a war is always a losing position. In U.S. history for the last century, polls that ask whether we should make a war that the President favors always produce a majority for the war. Always. To organize a movement to say no to a war that a President wants always loses. The President gets about 16 percent support out of deference to presidential authority, about 20 percent out of nationalistic support for our country against that enemy country, and about 20 percent out of response to the threat the President claims is there—the weapons of mass destruction, or the dominoes that will fall after Vietnam falls. The threat is seldom true, and almost always inflated, but it gets 20 percent support initially. The war becomes unpopular only after people see the pain, the cost, and the destructiveness of waging it. Just to say no is to guarantee failure.

Realism is clear: If we want majority support for a different action instead of war, we have to help people identify an alternative to war. People have to sense empowerment to do something effective about the alleged threat. That is what just peacemaking is about—identifying the alternatives.

JUST PEACEMAKING POINTS TO ALTERNATIVES THAT ARE EMPOWERING

Two just peacemaking practices are support for the United Nations and support for international networks of cooperation. We are stronger when we act together, and when we benefit from the wisdom of other nations as well as our own. When five polls asked if we should let the international inspections agency finish their work before making war on Iraq, we won and war lost by two to one in all five polls. When three polls asked if we should get support from the UN before making war on Iraq, we won and war lost by almost two to one. Just peacemaking identifies alternatives, and is more effective than "just say no." This is basic reality: people need the empowerment of seeing an alternative.

In my teaching I have experienced again and again that when students understand the alternatives offered by just peacemaking, then they support the criteria of just war or pacifism with far more energy, because they see what can be effective instead of making war. That will be true of your church members if you teach them just peacemaking practices.

Two just peacemaking practices are to support human rights and also work for just and sustainable economic development. When Turkey was faced with PKK terrorism seeking independence for Muslim Kurds, they attacked the terrorists militarily—and 30,000 people died. But then Turkey switched from militarily attacking the PKK terrorists to emphasizing human rights and economic development for the Kurds. This separated the Kurdish people from the terrorists; they saw they could do better supporting the government than supporting the terrorists. PKK terrorism in Turkey lost support and was abandoned. This was far more effective and empowering than the U.S. trying to end terrorism by making war on Iraq or the Russians making war on Chechnya!

When an extremist Muslim terrorist group, Al Qaeda, attacked the twin towers and the Pentagon on 9/11, the U.S. government could have asked about what was making those radical Muslims so angry, and taken action for human rights and economic development in the Middle East and Palestine, thereby separating Muslims from the terrorists. Instead, we were led in a violent response of revenge, announcing a permanent war on Muslim terrorism, plus a war on Afghanistan, plus a war on Iraq: three wars announced against Muslims in one Presidential term.

In 2003, there were 208 international terrorist attacks. But then the war on Iraq began. This, added on to the other wars declared on Muslims, and torture of Muslims, greatly increased anger and recruitment to terrorism. Here are the data, from the U.S. Counterterrorism Agency:

- 208 terrorist attacks caused 625 deaths in 2003;
- 3,168 attacks caused 1,907 deaths in 2004.
- 11,111 attacks caused 14,602 deaths in 2005.
- 14,371 attacks caused 13,186 deaths in 2006.
- 14,414 attacks caused 22,719 deaths in 2007.
- 11,662 attacks caused 15,708 deaths in 2008.
- 10,969 attacks caused 15,310 deaths in 2009.
- 11,604 attacks caused 13,186 deaths in 2010.

The economic cost of the Iraq and Afghanistan wars was two or three trillion dollars, depending on whether we include the medical costs after the wars and the interest payments on the added indebtedness that will go on and on for decades. How disempowering that still is!

Most authors of the just peacemaking paradigm also support just war theory. Some supported the war on Afghanistan. But I do not know any who supported the war on Iraq, or the torture.

Fortunately, when the rebellions of the Arab Spring broke forth in Tunisia, Egypt, and Libya, the U.S. government responded in a just peacemaking way. Just peacemaking theory says do not try to impose democracy by making war. Instead, support human rights and nonviolent direct action, which is the way democracy has spread in our time. The U.S. government pressed the Egyptian army to support the nonviolent movement for human rights, not to make war against it. Just peacemaking also says support the United Nations and international networks of cooperation. The U.S. government acted in Libya only with the urging of the League of Arab Nations, NATO, and the United Nations—not unilaterally. As a result, Arabs and Muslims are not angry at the U.S. for "imposing" these revolutions on Libya or other Arab nations. They rightly credit the Arab Spring to nonviolent direct action by Arabs, and to the push for human rights, and to restrained international support in Libya. Recruitment to terrorism has not jumped but decreased since then, and certainly has not jumped fifteen times as it did in 2004. Nor did our support for human rights lead to huge additional economic costs. It was effective, and it was supported internationally.

One of the empowering practices of just peacemaking is to foster just and sustainable economic development. As the National Priorities Project (www.nationalpriorities.org) points out, national security depends on economic security. Out-of-control military spending is threatening our economic security. The National Priorities Project compares how our two parties differ on military spending plans.

I am not saying the Obama administration is perfect from a just peacemaking perspective. But in his Nobel Peace Prize address, President Obama mentioned just war only three times and mentioned only three of the just war criteria; but he mentioned just peace four times, and advocated all ten of the just peacemaking practices. His response to the Arab Spring has been far closer to just peacemaking's practices of supporting nonviolent direct action, human rights, international cooperation, the United Nations and international organizations.

His response to Iran has included conflict resolution—actual negotiations—for the first time since 1979. Similarly, former president Carter actually negotiated with North Korea and achieved a halt to nuclear enrichment there until the Bush Administration broke off negotiations. By contrast, we have seen that the refusal of several Administrations to practice conflict resolution with Iran, and the refusal of the Bush Administration to talk with North Korea for six years, was not effective but disempowering.

The tenth practice of just peacemaking is to encourage grassroots peacemaking groups. In September 2012, representatives from several denominations' peace fellowships, and from Sojourners and Every Church a Peace Church, met to organize a movement for developing just peacemaking groups in congregations—with an inward journey of study and listening prayer, and an outward journey of supporting just peacemaking practices. It will be centered in the six-member staff of the Church of the Brethren's Living Peace Church, and supported by several other church organizations. We invite you to join our process of empowering church groups to make their Christian witness by developing just peacemaking groups in churches. We will be using a revised and much updated edition of the little book I wrote thirty years ago for the Southern Baptist Brotherhood Commission, *The Journey Into Peacemaking.* This will be empowering for those church members who care about following Jesus in peacemaking.

The effectiveness of just peacemaking is basic biblical truth. Isaiah 32:16 says:

> Then justice will dwell in the wilderness,
> And delivering justice abide in the fruitful field;
> The effect of delivering justice will be peace,
> And the result of delivering justice quietness and trust forever
> (author's translation).

We need to translate the Hebrew *tsedaqah* as "delivering justice." In our culture of possessive individualism, if we translate it as "righteousness," we make people think of individualistic righteousness that we can possess. That's self-righteousness. Look how *tsedaqah* functions in the Hebrew scriptures: it is always relational, not individualistic. It is often in parallel with *mishpat*, justice. It is deliverance for the oppressed and marginalized, and never punishment.

The ineffectiveness of not knowing the practices that are effective for making peace is why Jesus weeps over Jerusalem (Luke 19:42–44). They do not know the practices "that make for peace. But now they are hidden from your eyes. . . . Your enemies will . . . set up a siege around you and . . . will crush you to the ground, you and your children within you, and they will not leave within you one stone upon another" (author's translation).

Six times in the Gospels Jesus prophesied the destruction of Jerusalem, and his prophecies came true. The Israelite leaders knew only blame and resentment against the Romans, and did not know the practices of just peacemaking that God in Christ was showing them. That ignorance of the practices that make for peace brought about the destruction of Jerusalem and exile from the land.

THE LONG ROAD OF SLOW REPENTANCE

Our nation, and yes, many of our church members, have been so influenced to trust in horses and chariots, and nuclear weapons, and making many wars, as the source of our security, that it will be a long process to shift the culture slowly toward the practices that make for peace.

Let me state clearly my respect, love, and appreciation for our fellow Americans in the armed services who have sacrificed enormous self-discipline and hard work, distance from home and families, risk of death, life-lasting wounds both bodily and mental, and too often actual death, for wars they did not choose. I think of my student Jake Diliberto, who was in the first Marine unit to fight in Afghanistan, who fought twice in Iraq, and who has since provided leadership to Rethink Afghanistan. And my own father, who resigned as Governor of Minnesota in order to enter the Navy in World War II, whose ship was torpedoed and sunk; we deeply mourned his death, only to learn that he had survived. He ended the war as a much-decorated captain in the Navy. He came back deeply committed to preventing another war like that, because he saw how horrible war was, and he strongly supported the just peacemaking paradigm. I honor them. But as Jake says, it does not properly honor those who fought in Iraq to say "they fought for our freedom." This is false use of their sacrifices to propound a militaristic ideology that our freedom is based on making war more than on our commitment to human rights. Iraq was no threat to our freedom. It was a threat to the ideological misconceptions of those who decided on that war against the advice of three-fourths of the United Nations Security Council.

Because of the power behind that ideology, as David Gushee says, it will be a long process to shift the churches and the culture slowly to the practices that make for peace. But we are contributing to that shift. Our *Just Peacemaking* book is now already in its third edition; our *Interfaith Just Peacemaking*, with ten leading Muslim and ten leading Jewish as well as Christian authors will soon be published in paperback; our *Formation for Life: Just Peacemaking* is also in print. Just peacemaking theory is now commonly cited in books, articles, and websites, and all its ten practices have been endorsed by the President and are partially transforming policies. You can make a difference in your churches and in your teaching and in your advocacy. We are gradually turning a significant portion of Christians around. You can be empowered to participate.

JUST PEACEMAKING IS BASED ON FAITHFULNESS TO A THICKER JESUS

I have focused on the effectiveness and empowerment of just peacemaking practices, because that is what David Gushee was yearning for in his opening essay, and because so many evangelicals have been led astray by the Platonic idealism that assumes peacemaking is only an ideal. Peacemaking is not an ahistorical ideal; it is an effective set of practices in real history.

But I hope we are all clear that just peacemaking is not only about effectiveness; the just peacemaking practices arose out of an effort to be faithful to Jesus' teachings in the Sermon on the Mount. The Sermon on the Mount is not a bunch of Platonic ideals. It is God's will. I make that clear in my initial book, *Just Peacemaking: Transforming Initiatives for Justice and Peace*, and my new book, *A Thicker Jesus*. You can see the rooting of just peacemaking in Jesus' teaching in the following summary of the ten just peacemaking practices.

Initiatives

1. *Support nonviolent direct action.* This practice is based on Jesus' way of transforming initiatives (Matt 5:38–42). Go the second mile, give both your cloak and coat, turn the other cheek, and give to the person who begs. It is proving widely effective, as in the U.S. civil rights movement, East Germany, Poland, the Philippines, Iran, Tunisia, and Egypt. Now Palestinians on the West Bank are adopting it (see the movie *Budrus*). By contrast, how smart was it for Hamas to engage

in suicide bombing, and then to lob rockets into Israel, thus driving Israeli politics to the militaristic right and providing justification for the massive Israeli war against Gaza and locking the Gazans in like a prison?

2. *Take independent initiatives to reduce threat* (also rooted in Matthew 5:38–42). This practice involves taking a series of visible and verifiable actions, not waiting for the slow process of negotiations, announcing the purpose as decreasing threat and distrust, inviting reciprocation; not leaving the initiator weak, announcing the timing in advance, and carrying it out on time. This is how the Nuclear Freeze Campaign got the Soviet Union and NATO to get rid of all medium-range nuclear missiles, and thus to move toward ending the Cold War, and how George H. W. Bush and Soviet Premier Mikhail Gorbachev got rid of half the superpower nuclear arsenals.

3. *Use cooperative conflict resolution.* This practice is based on Matthew 5:21–26, where Jesus teaches us to go make peace with the adversary while there's time. How smart was it for several U.S. administrations to refuse to negotiate with Iran, and for the Bush Administration to refuse to negotiate with North Korea, instead threatening their survival, thus disempowering the U.S. from preventing them from developing nuclear weapons? Instead we should have taken the initiative to at least attempt cooperative conflict resolution.

4. *Acknowledge responsibility for conflict and injustice and seek repentance and forgiveness.* This practice is based on Matthew 7:1–5. It was initiated by Dietrich Bonhoeffer, and then German churches, and then by Germany to begin to make amends after World War II. It has been undertaken by some U.S. and state governments in relation to our own wrongdoing, by the Truth and Reconciliation Commission in South Africa, and some other nations—all in efforts to lance festering historical resentments by telling the truth about national wrongdoing in a spirit of repentance and quest for forgiveness.

Justice (Based on Matthew 6:19–33)

5. *Advance human rights, religious liberty, and democracy.* Pushing for human rights, a key aspect of justice, has helped change most Latin American and Eastern European countries and several Asian

countries from dictatorships to democracies. No democracy with human rights made war against another democracy with human rights in the entire twentieth century. This works; it spreads peace.

6. *Foster just and sustainable economic development.* Relative economic deprivation is a powerful cause of civil war, insurgencies, and terrorism. This practice is a critically important preventive measure.

Love: Include Enemies in the Community of Neighbors

7. *Work with emerging cooperative forces in the international system.* This practice as well as the next one are based on Matthew 5:43–48, where Jesus teaches us to love our enemies.

8. *Strengthen the United Nations and international efforts for cooperation and human rights.* Empirical evidence shows that the more that nations are involved in international organizations, communication, travel, missions, international business, and the United Nations, the less frequently they make war or suffer from war. Unilateral policies cause more wars.

9. *Reduce offensive weapons and weapons trade.* This practice is based on Matthew 26:52, where Jesus tells us to put away our swords. A nation with overwhelming offensive weapons is tempted to use them: Serbia against Bosnia, Croatia, and Kosovo; the U.S. in 2001–2003. These nations declared three wars each—much to their regret. Instead we should reduce the global weapons trade, with special attention to offensive weapons.

10. *Encourage grassroots peacemaking groups and voluntary associations.* This is based on Jesus' strategy of developing a group of disciples and planting groups in various villages. Consider also Paul's travels and letters developing churches. Now Living Peace Church and Every Church a Peace Church are organizing congregational just peacemaking groups.

My fundamental claim in this chapter is that just peacemaking practices are both empowering for Christian disciples and effective in international relations. No discussion of evangelical engagement with issues of peace and war is adequate without serious consideration of just peacemaking.

5 The World Evangelical Alliance and Christ's Call to Peacemaking

Geoff Tunnicliffe

I WANT TO COMMEND all who have written for this book and participated in the original September 2012 conference on evangelical peacemaking. We in the World Evangelical Alliance believe this work is a direct response to Jesus' call for us to be peacemakers and ambassadors of reconciliation.

I am a fellow Christian pilgrim seeking to live out my faith in Christ and be obedient to my Lord. My journey has included serving as a missionary, church planter, evangelist, aid worker, executive, and consultant. For the last seven years I have had the immense privilege of serving as the Secretary General of the World Evangelical Alliance.

As I travel the world on behalf of our global family I am regularly confronted with the reality and deadly consequences of conflict. The truth is that I have seen far too many tragic results of strife and anger. I have been in too many refugee camps. I have held too many children who have been orphaned. I have sat with too many widows weeping over the loss of their husbands.

At a press conference at the United Nations during the arms trade treaty negotiations, I was asked why the illegal arms trade was an important topic for evangelicals.

My response: as a global community of 600 million Christians, our churches are confronted daily with the impact of illegal weapons

- Our hospitals treat the victims of violence.

- Our church leaders counsel the traumatized.

- All forms of conflict negatively impact our development programs.

- Our aid agencies seek to care for and rehabilitate child soldiers.

- Our inner city communities are confronted with the outcomes of gang warfare.

For all of us who say we are followers of Jesus, as we observe or experience the brokenness of our world, it should break our hearts. If we feel the pain so deeply, I can't imagine what our loving God feels. The One who is called the Prince of Peace. The One who laid down his life, so that we could be reconciled to God and each other.

For over 160 years, the World Evangelical Alliance has had a rich history of seeking to build unity as we respond biblically to the issues of the day. Today, the WEA stands alongside the two other world Christian bodies, the Catholic Church and the World Council of Churches.

With a membership of 129 national alliances along with the largest evangelical networks, denominations, and agencies, we seek to be God's messengers of hope and peace. At the center of our community are the millions of local churches that touch almost every part of the planet.

Believing the local church is God's primary instrument of transformation, we seek to serve our global family by equipping leaders for national impact, speak as a trusted voice, and facilitate a connecting hub for synergy and great kingdom impact.

In the last number of years we have built upon our strong commitment to theology, religious liberty, and global mission. We have launched initiatives related to human trafficking, the millennium development goals, creation care, nuclear weapons, and peace and reconciliation. Just recently we appointed Salvation Army Commissioner Christine MacMillan as our Senior Advisor for Social Justice.

As one of the three world church bodies, the WEA is frequently asked by governments, Christian leaders and other faith communities to engage some of the most challenging issues on our planet. While many of our activities are very public, a significant part of our work is accomplished by what has been described as track 2 or track 1.5 diplomacy, quietly working behind the scenes.

Our engagement builds on the rich traditions of evangelicals who have devoted themselves to being instruments of social change and transformation.

One of my personal heroes is the British Member of Parliament, William Wilberforce, who along with other evangelical activists ended the slave trade in the British Empire. I am also reminded of evangelicals who worked both privately and publicly to end apartheid in South Africa or promote civil rights in the U.S.

In recent times, the WEA has been active on a number of fronts in seeking to bring peace and reconciliation.

In 2011, we sent referendum monitors to South Sudan in support of a free and fair vote for independence. In April 2012 we were able to bring together tribal leaders, chiefs, and politicians from Jongelei State in South Sudan.

After the independence of South Sudan in 2011, violent conflict broke out between several tribes in this new nation, leaving thousands dead. For three days, these leaders, many of them Christian, wrestled with how to bring peace to their region. While much remains to be done, we are encouraged by a dramatic decrease in violence since the peace summit.

As the civil war was ending in Sri Lanka, we took an international delegation to this war-ravaged country, meeting not only with church leaders, but leaders of other faiths and the government. Again, our goal was to help in discovering long-term resolutions to the conflict. In Sri Lanka, as in other countries, the church is at the heart of the solution to ethnic conflict. In Sri Lanka the church is really the only body that has significant numbers of both Tamils and Sinhalese. The church itself has demonstrated that these ethnic communities can live together in peace. Today, we continue to work with our sisters and brothers in Sri Lanka as they persist under great oppression to find peaceful solutions to their current societal conflicts.

In July 2012, during the arms trade talks at the UN, it was Bishop Taban, the president of our Evangelical Alliance in South Sudan, who was selected to represent the entire NGO community in presenting the 650,000 signatures to Secretary General Ban Ki Moon. Bishop Taban gave a powerfully moving testimony of how at two hours of age he was on the run in the arms of his mother fleeing gunfire. At twelve years of age he became a child soldier, finally ending up in the liberation army as an arms procurement officer. Having experienced firsthand for all four decades of his life the impact of conflict, he is one of the leading voices for building peace in the newest nation on earth.

As the Arab Spring impacted Egypt we worked closely with Christian leaders as they sought to guide churches in how best to engage in nonviolent responses to their volatile context.

Over the last several years we have sought to assist in the ongoing Israeli-Palestinian conflict. We accepted into membership the Palestinian Evangelical Body to stand alongside our long-time member, the Evangelical Alliance of Israel. We appointed a Holy Land ambassador with the goal of building bridges of peace and understanding.

While any engagement by evangelicals in this long-term conflict results in controversy, we must not be intimidated into backing away from promoting peace, reconciliation, and justice.

With growing clashes in Nigeria and attacks against churches we are seeking how we can contribute to a process that will end the violence.

As WEA, we believe we must find ways of working with all the actors in resolving conflict. This includes leaders of other faiths. It is my privilege to serve as the first evangelical in the role of the co-president of Religions for Peace (www.religionsforpeace.org). This engagement has already led to situations where we can work for peace together.

While some in our community may question this kind of interaction, we must recognize that we have a strong biblical mandate to promote peace building and join others in building more harmonious societies.

Let me give you a very personal example. Most people are aware that a pastor of a tiny church in Florida wanted to burn a stack of Korans. Initially we decided not to respond, not wanting to give oxygen to this "silly" story. However, as international media began to bring focus to this story, we began to receive requests from Christian leaders around the world to engage. In addition, senior political leaders began to ask for our intervention.

We took up the call. We reached out to this pastor and challenged him to reconsider this senseless stunt that would provoke radicals to respond with violence. In that conversation, the pastor from Florida proposed that he would not burn the Korans if a New York City imam would not build a mosque near Ground Zero. Believing that this sort of quid pro quo negotiation would only lead to further conflicted situations, we sought other remedies.

I called my good friend, Jim Wallis, the leader of Sojourners. As we talked about the situation, Jim asked where I was located. I told him I was in New York City. Jim said he was amazed, as he had just been discussing my name with Imam Feisal in NYC.

That telephone conversation led to an introduction to Imam Feisal, who in 2012 was named one of the hundred most influential people in the world by *Time* magazine.

The introduction by Jim led to the beginning of what has become a wonderful friendship with Imam Feisal. Through our journey together we have discovered that we have a shared commitment to promoting peace, working together for the common good, and advancing religious freedom for all. Together with our wives we have spent time in each other's homes building our relationship. We have appeared on international TV and radio programs together promoting peace and reconciliation.

Together, we have been saying that even though we come from very different faith traditions we can work together for peace.

When speaking at Yale University to a group of Christian, Muslim and Jewish leaders, Daisy Khan, Imam Feisal's wife, publicly commended WEA for speaking out for religious freedom for all faiths. This shocked some of the imams and led to a protracted discussion on how the imams could help Christian minorities in their contexts.

Most of you may be aware of the tragic story from Pakistan of Rimshah Masih, the eleven-year-old Christian girl with Down Syndrome who was arrested on blasphemy charges. This of course created great outrage in the global Christian community and human rights groups.

Our feeling was that it would be far more powerful if Muslim groups condemned this action. We contacted Imam Feisal and leaders of other Muslim groups, asking for their help. Imam Feisal wrote a powerful letter to Pakistani political leaders not only condemning the charges on humanitarian grounds but also by Islamic teaching. Daisy Khan wrote an op-ed piece for the *Huffington Post*, and other Muslim groups used other mediums to communicate their outrage.

What are the results of these kinds of encounters? We will never fully know. We just know it's the right thing to do. However, it is encouraging to hear reports arriving that describe the positive impact of our work.

I was attending a meeting in Geneva several months after our intervention with the Koran burning. A member of the royal family of one of the countries in the Middle East, whom I had become acquainted with, came up and thanked me for what we did. He said, "Your actions probably saved hundreds of lives."

While we thank God for what we have been able to accomplish, we recognize so much more needs to be done. That is why we launched our Peace and Reconciliation Initiative.

We want to say loudly that we evangelicals want to be on the forefront of peace building. I am so grateful for the tremendous leadership of this initiative by New Zealander Steve Tollestrup. However, for WEA, our peace building and reconciliation work is not limited to this one initiative. We recognize that other parts of WEA directly and indirectly work on issues of peace. We are working hard on building our internal synergies between our various commissions and initiatives and our engagement at the United Nations. I keep telling our staff and leaders that all the easy jobs have been done. It's just the tough ones that are left. It requires clear vision and internal alignment to face these challenges.

However, it is going to take much greater partnership within the Christian community. We are thankful for our partnership with the Lausanne movement. We are also grateful for our collaboration with the two other world Christian communities, the Catholic Church and the World Council of Churches.

In 2011, after five years of animated discussions, the WEA, the Vatican, and the WCC signed a joint document on "Christian Witness in a Multi-Religious World." The three bodies had never before signed a joint statement on any issue. This powerful joint statement specifically speaks to the issue of inter-faith conflict and violence. Even though it has just been in circulation for a few years, we are already encouraged by promising results being reported.

This kind of cooperation is just the tip of the iceberg. We can do so much more. We must do so much more together.

However, we must recognize there is often a cost to being a peacemaker. For some that cost is the ultimate sacrifice.

I think of my friend Shabhaz Bhatti, who was the first Christian appointed to a cabinet position in the Pakistan government. In his responsibilities as Minister of Minorities he spoke out for religious minorities and the disenfranchised. He was a champion of human rights. However, at heart he was a peacemaker and committed to finding ways that Pakistanis could live in peace with each other.

I remember having a private dinner with Shabhaz in Washington. In the course of our dialogue he described his strategy for developing interfaith peace councils in hundreds of communities across Pakistan. It was a bold vision. I assured him of our support. Our conversation turned more sobering. Shabhaz calmly informed me that a few days before we met, the leader of Al Qaeda had warned him that if he did not stop his work he was number one on their hit list.

I looked Shabhaz in the eye and said, "You don't have to put your life at risk." With a quiet confidence, he replied, "This is my calling. This is what Jesus has asked me to do."

About a month later, I had just returned from a trip and checked my email. There was an email from Shabhaz, outlining a strategy for us to visit Pakistan to meet with the President and religious leaders. I discovered later that this was one of his last communications. Along with the details of our trip he wrote: "I personally believe that it is Jesus Christ who has once again bestowed unto me this responsibility and position with a special purpose and mission to serve the suffering humanity and I am determined to carry on defending the principles of religious freedom, human equality, social justice and the rights of minorities."

Early the next morning, I received a telephone call to inform me Shabhaz had been assassinated as he was driving the few blocks from his home to the parliament.

For us, we may not lose our lives in our efforts in peacemaking; however, make no mistake about it, there will be a price to pay.

With this reality in mind let us move ahead in faith and courage.

This book, and the earlier conference, are strong signs that we as evangelicals are committed to working together with those inside and outside our community for the good of all. We are committed to following the admonishment of scripture to be peacemakers and ambassadors of reconciliation. For as Paul wrote:

> Therefore, if anyone is in Christ, the new creation has come: The old has gone, the new is here! All this is from God, who reconciled us to himself through Christ and gave us the ministry of reconciliation: that God was reconciling the world to himself in Christ, not counting people's sins against them. And he has committed to us the message of reconciliation. We are therefore Christ's ambassadors, as though God were making his appeal through us. (2 Cor 5:17–19, NIV)

May God empower us through the work of his Spirit to be his ambassadors of peace and reconciliation.

6 The Peace Witness of the Fellowship of Reconciliation

MARK C. JOHNSON

IT IS A PRIVILEGE to be asked to introduce you to the Fellowship of Reconciliation (FOR), a community of practice that many of you will know in passing and some more intimately. FOR is America's oldest interfaith, multi-cultural peace organization. Founded in Germany in 1914 on the platform of the Konstanz train terminal, and established in the United States in 1915 through the impetus of the ubiquitous John R. Mott of the World Student Christian Movement and the YMCA, it is a reminder that this work of peacemaking is not new in the world.

A seminal part of the early twentieth century evangelical call of the Great Commission, to bring all to Christ in that first generation of the century, FOR became first ecumenical and then interfaith earlier, and more uniquely, than perhaps any other fellowship of Christians in the early years of global evangelism. With branches in over fifty-five countries around the world, the International Fellowship of Reconciliation has long been a global presence. Founded in the belief that love and truth are critical to and capable of resolving conflict, it is a profoundly evangelical movement, with roots also feeding the work from Thoreau to Tolstoy, from Gandhi to King.

These days it seems that the work of justice advocacy is syncopated with the cycles of the natural world, September serving as the season of rebirth of the work of peace and justice after a long summer of sleepy re-generation. But that is simply a bit of metaphorical conceit. Like the work of the gospel, spreading the Good News, the work of political advocacy for peace and justice is the work of all seasons.

This is never clearer than in that quadrennial cycle of presidential elections in this country when the choices we make, based on our values and grounded in our faith, bring us face to face with Caesar once more, as Caesar seeks to secure our loyalty again to his vision of the kingdom of peace on earth.

When I was first invited to reflect on the work of FOR for this volume I found myself rather quickly confounded by the absence of a clear articulation of the work of reconciliation in our history, though reconciliation is the principle and practice from which our very name is derived. There was actually very little good articulation of reconciliation in the FOR archive, despite the profound impact and relevance of the work of reconciliation throughout our history. Often when I have addressed audiences on the topics of pacifism and reconciliation I have been dismissed as archaic and irrelevant, utopian and old-fashioned at the same time.

But during the last few years, the rising affirmation of "just peacemaking," the growing voice of an evangelical call to peacemaking and creation care, and the superb contribution of Daniel Philpott and his colleagues on religion and global political reconciliation,[1] a vacuum has been filled to my nearly total satisfaction.

To simply summarize Philpott's contribution let us stipulate that, as his titles make clear, the role of religion is resurgent in global politics in the twenty-first century, and an ethic of reconciliation is a profoundly important contribution that religious thought and practices make to a peaceful future. Philpott's delineation of the practices of reconciliation accurately define the work of FOR as an advocate for:

1. building socially just institutions and relations between states

2. acknowledgement of injury

3. reparations for harms done

4. punishment for crimes committed

5. apology for injuries inflicted

6. forgiveness.

FOR, like much of the peace and justice movement, finds itself called to this work by the Old Testament, speaking with a prophetic voice, speaking truth to power, reminding the peoples that the work of liberation is not yet complete, that the captives have not yet been freed, that the blind cannot

1. Philpott, Toft, and Shah, *God's Century*; Philpott, *Just and Unjust Peace*.

yet see, that the hungry are not yet fed, the naked clothed, the innocent protected, evil contained.

We are the peace-builders, meek perhaps, but we will not be quiet, nor should we be. Neither the press nor the President listens to the silence or even to the still small voice of resistance and conscience; it is the prophets and the teachers of all traditions, the rabbis, the preachers and the imams, that call us out nonetheless, whose voices we continue to amplify.

I could rehearse the highlights of nearly one hundred years of faith-based active nonviolence exercised to secure a right relationship among all peoples and the earth on the part of the Fellowship of Reconciliation. Let me instead offer a somewhat rapturous and poetic litany of just one week in September 2012 to illustrate how this coalition of forty-five chapters and sixty-five affiliates, including more than a dozen religious and community-based peace fellowships and affiliates, works to seek and build the Beloved Community, to live together in the World House.

During the week of September 4, 2012, Rabbi Lynn Gottlieb, forty-year FOR member and founder of Shomer Shalom Network for Jewish Nonviolence, a new Jewish peace fellowship established for the study of the Torah of nonviolence, took an FOR delegation of muralists to the three West Bank Palestinian refugee camps as a part of the Arts of Resistance. Their goal was to join young Palestinian school children as they paint murals of their aspirations for a better world on the walls of their schools and the streets of their camps. Typically these will be visions of swimming in the sea, harvesting olives, or playing football, not their reality of long lines at check points to pass through eighteen-foot walls, brothers and fathers in prisons for opposing occupation, or fishermen denied access to the sea at their feet by belligerent superpowers. This delegation to the West Bank is in keeping with many decades of civilian diplomacy to nations living under the threat of war or in the midst of conflict. FOR began this practice with visits to Russia in 1917 and continues today with regular delegations to Colombia and Iran and co-sponsors travels to Afghanistan and Israel/Palestine. When delegates return they are frequently interviewed in local media as new "experts" and they gravitate to the halls of Congress to share their newly won insights and concerns about abuses of human rights and a path to peace.

Several days later, Washington D.C. "welcomed" over one hundred "Caravanistas" as the last stop for the month-long tour of the Caravan for Peace with Justice and Dignity. Originating in Mexico, two buses traveled to twenty-seven cities in the United States carrying families of the victims of the drug war, a war fought with American arms effectively to protect the access of American addicts to cocaine and marijuana at the expense of the lives of innocents in Mexico and throughout Latin America, as well as in the inner cities of the United States. Tens of thousands of people have been slaughtered in the past six years alone, only to prolong civil unrest and injustice, anti-unionism, and pro-imperialism. These survivors on the Caravan have traveled to join FOR, the Presbyterian Peace Fellowship, the Episcopal Peace Fellowship and others in calling on churches across the southwest to "Heed God's Call" and close down the unregulated exchange of guns through straw man sales that end up in Mexico to be used in massacres. They have stood in witness in front of City Halls, State Capitals and the halls of the U.S. Congress to protest and witness.

For the past ten years FOR volunteers have lived and served in protective accompaniment to an agrarian peace community of more than half a dozen villages in San Jose de Apartado, Colombia. There, in Colombia, the impact of a civil war of more than forty years duration, funded in significant measure by the growing and cartelization of cocaine and marijuana, has been deadly. And in recent years the waves of bloody violence have rolled through Mexico. The current Caravan for Peace is but one manifestation of education about this issue led by FOR. Previous visitors have been invited onto the floor of the California Legislature to describe the carnage in Mexico as part of an appeal to turn the money for drug interdiction to the work of drug addiction in the U.S., and the expenditures on arms and munitions to the service of education and health. Other representatives of FOR's work in Colombia and Mexico now travel to local communities throughout the United States with this message.

Also during the same week, FOR's communications staff and Middle East Task Force team worked with our National Chapter for Global Days of Listening, our allies at Kathy Kelly's Voices for Creative Nonviolence, and with Shane Claiborne at The Simple Way, to launch a new web site for the Afghan Peace Volunteers.[2] Once a month for four years this precious group of Afghan youth have convened a global conference call in which young people who live in the midst of conflict from Mexico to Malaysia, from Afghanistan to Gaza, from Sri Lanka to Sudan, talk to one another to give comfort and encouragement as they seek to wake the world to the horrors of their lives in war zones and their dreams for peace and justice.

2. Websites: http://globaldaysoflistening.org/; http://www.2millionfriends.org/.

The website has initiated a call for two million friends of peace around the world.

On the eve of President Obama's inauguration in 2009 this small group of boys dedicated a Peace Park in Bamiyan during a visit by Ambassador Karl Eikenberry. They sent a short video message to the President, the first of nearly 150 such videos appearing on their website—Our Journey to Smile/Why Not Love—over the past four years.[3] Today they inspire us anew and drive a community of peace-builders to rededicate ourselves to the work of peace every day.

Virtually all of FOR's work seeks to give individuals the skills and the courage of their convictions, of their conscience, to practice their faith in seeking to correct ills in their own hearts, their families and communities, and their nation that will bring peace and justice, dignity and humanity, security and sanctity to their lives and times, yes, our lives and times. For a more complete sense of our work and history you can visit our website: www.forusa.org. It is an ongoing effort to be present in the public space seeking to clarify and support our moral responsibility to be peace-makers for all peoples and nations.

I close with this pivotally important prophetic text, Isaiah 58:6–9:

> What I'm interested in seeing you do is:
> sharing your food with the hungry,
> inviting the homeless poor into your homes,
> putting clothes on the shivering ill-clad,
> being available to your own families.
> Do this and the lights will turn on,
> and your lives will turn around at once.
> Your righteousness will pave your way.
> The God of glory will secure your passage.
> Then when you pray, God will answer.
> You'll call out for help and I'll say, "Here I am." (The Message)

---

3. http://www.youtube.com/user/ourjourneytosmile.

7 Christian Peacemaking and Witness with Muslims

Joseph Cumming

I HAVE THE PRIVILEGE of directing the Reconciliation Program at the Yale Center for Faith and Culture. This role opens doors for me to work with Muslim leaders from around the world—leaders such as the Grand Imam of Al-Azhar, Shiʻi ayatollahs in Iran, and the head of the thirty-million-strong Muhammadiyah movement in Indonesia.

My work in September 2012 involved a video called "The Innocence of Muslims," which was posted on social media sites, sparking protests and violence across the Muslim world. As an example of what my role at Yale allows me to do, I worked closely with Leith Anderson, president of the National Association of Evangelicals (NAE), to craft a press release from the NAE about the video. I sent the press release, together with a statement of my own, to my personal contacts at the Al-Jazeera news network. Though Al-Jazeera was trying to cover the topic in a balanced way, they kept calling the video "the offensive American film." This fueled anti-American violence. I sent them an email asking them to refer to the video as "the offensive film," leaving out the word "American," and asking them to emphasize the voices of Muslim leaders who were urging restraint and nonviolence. Al Jazeera immediately changed their coverage, taking the word "American" out of their broadcast. In this way, partnership with influential Muslims helped prevent additional violence.

In the spring of 2002, I was invited to meet with Sheikh Fadlallah, who was probably the most influential Shiʻi ayatollah in the Arab world. He was sometimes described in the American media as the "spiritual head of Hezbollah." That is not entirely accurate, but certainly his anti-American credentials have been well-established. We requested a meeting with him on the day before 'Ashura, which is the holiest day of the year for Shi'a, so he was very busy. His secretary scheduled us for a two-minute audience. We would take thirty seconds to shake hands for the television cameras, and he would speak first, so I had to think and pray carefully about what I would say during the few remaining seconds.

As I was on my way to that meeting with him, driving through South Beirut, I saw a banner over the street that said in Arabic, "Victory of blood over the sword." This refers to the Shi'i Imam Husayn, whose death is commemorated on 'Ashura. When his enemies came to kill him, according to Shi'i belief, God showed Imam Husayn that he could take up arms and kill his enemies, but instead, he voluntarily laid down his sword and allowed his enemies to kill him, thereby gaining a position of intercession for the forgiveness of sins. In my thirty seconds to speak to Sheikh Fadlallah, I told him about the banner and what I understood the phrase to mean to the Shi'a. I said, "That's what I believe about Jesus—that when his enemies came to kill him, Jesus said he could ask God for a legion of angels to kill his enemies, but instead, he laid down his life in love, praying for the forgiveness of those enemies. I believe that is the key to breaking the cycle of violence and hatred in the world."

One might have expected Sheikh Fadlallah to respond that Muslims do not believe in Jesus' death on the cross, but he had just read an article that I wrote in which I laid out from the Qur'an and the Hadith and the Islamic exegetical tradition why there is a legitimate minority view within the Muslim community that Jesus did die and rise again. Sheikh Fadlallah turned to his followers and said, "I totally agree with every word this Christian man of God has just said."

I then said, "Okay, my two minutes are up. Thank you very much."

He insisted I stay, and we spoke for two hours. He wanted to ask me about everything from whether Christians worship three gods to the Israeli-Palestinian conflict.

The day before I met with him, the Israelis, with an American-made helicopter and American-made missiles, had been trying to kill a militant Hamas activist, but instead, they had accidentally killed two innocent boys who had been playing soccer in the street. That night, television screens across the Arab world showed the mangled bodies of these two innocent boys beside a statement by an American televangelist. The televangelist had gone on television that day and said, "We totally support the Israeli Defense Forces in this legitimate act of self-defense." Sheikh Fadlallah asked me what I had to say about this as a Christian.

I answered, "I look at this the way I look at all suffering of innocent victims of violence, bigotry, and oppression—through the lens of the suffering and death of Jesus Christ. If it weren't for Jesus, I might think God had abandoned the human race, but in Jesus I see God's solidarity with all innocent victims of discrimination and violence and oppression." Sheikh Fadlallah appreciated my response very much.

A little over a year later, the Abu Ghraib scandal broke. Across the Arab world there were images of Iraqis being tortured by Americans, and Muslims were asking their religious leaders how they should respond. Hezbollah, under the influence of Sheikh Fadlallah, put together a video montage for their television station, in which they took images of Americans torturing Iraqis and spliced them together with images and music from the movie *The Passion of the Christ*. They issued a statement saying, "The suffering of Jesus Christ is a universal theme. It is something everyone, including us as Muslims, believes in."

Mel Gibson owned the copyright to that material, and this was a copyright violation, so he issued a cease-and-desist letter. Fortunately, his theological advisor, Father Bill Fulco, was a Yale graduate whom I knew through my work, and I was able to call Father Fulco and ask him to talk to Mr. Gibson about the issue. As a result, Mel Gibson decided to allow the broadcast. Because of this, for millions of Muslims, the way they looked at the Abu Ghraib scandal was in terms of Jesus' suffering and death for the world.

I want to thank every evangelical Christian who advocates for peace. Such evangelicals make possible the kind of work I do with Muslim leaders. Muslims generally perceive Christianity to be the most militaristic religion in the world, and they perceive America to be the most militaristic nation in the world. When I want to tell Muslims that Jesus is the Prince of Peace, it rings hollow if there are no other Christians standing for peace. On the other hand, when I can say that there are many evangelical Christians in America who are concerned for peace, standing up courageously for peace, and speaking out for peace, that lends tremendous credibility to my work with Muslim leaders.

Evangelicals who work for peace make my work possible by advocating for peacemaking in the Christian community. Evangelical Christians sometimes fear that building bridges with Muslims is part of a slippery slope toward one world religion and away from Christ. It is important that there are Christian voices that change the tone of the discourse in American evangelicalism so that it becomes possible for me to have constructive conversations with Muslims without being opposed by my brothers and sisters in Christ.

There is an important relationship between peacemaking and loving witness to Jesus Christ. Many people in the world think that one either works for peace or bears witness for Christ, but not both. In the aftermath of 9/11, two categories of books came out on the Christian book market about Islam and Muslims. One category advocated loving Muslims, building bridges and relationships, practicing hospitality, and reaching out with the love of Christ. The other category screamed that Muslims are a threat, that Islam is a threat, and that we have to defend ourselves against Muslims.

If you look at the authors of those books, the authors who speak about love are those who have lived and worked among Muslims, perhaps for decades, as my wife and I lived in North Africa for fifteen years. These authors have learned Muslims' languages, been in Muslims' homes, had Muslims in their homes, and shared meals with them. The authors who promote bigotry and fear are people who do not have Muslim friends or experience with Muslims.

I am concerned that in American evangelicalism today and, to a lesser extent, evangelicalism around the world, there is a split developing between two camps. One is the camp that has been influenced by people who advocate peacemaking, but who do not talk much about witness to Muslims. The other camp is the people who are denouncing the evils of Islam, and who are promoting fear of Muslims. These groups who teach fear of Muslims are sometimes, ironically, the ones who promote missions to Muslims. The young people who are being taught to work toward peace are not being encouraged to go out as witnesses. Those who are being encouraged toward missions are coming from churches that do not teach them to love Muslims. I am concerned that we may send out a generation of missionaries who do more harm than good, and that we may produce a generation of young people who could do great good, but who are not being encouraged to wed witness to their peacemaking. I urge the church to learn to keep witness and peacemaking together.

People are listening to us about peacemaking and reconciliation. We need to remind them that bearing witness to faith in Jesus is an important thing to do. It is important to Jesus; it is important to God. For those who are currently learning to be afraid of Muslims, we need to help them understand that if they want to reach out as missionaries to Muslims, they will need to make friendships with Muslims and to rethink the basis of their relationship to Muslims. In this way, we can help raise up a generation of Christians who are building their witness and their peacemaking on a foundation of love rather than fear.

8 U.S. Foreign Policy and the Muslim World

DOUGLAS M. JOHNSTON JR.

IF I HAD TO convey a single message to U.S. foreign policy practitioners, it would be that religion matters. For good or for ill, the world is growing increasingly religious. What's more, the nature of religion in many places is changing; it is becoming more dynamic, more activist, and more political. While the majority of religious movements are peaceful, some errant ideologies are at work justifying and encouraging violence. These ideologies must be countered, and countered effectively. Military force is clearly an asset in the fight against religious extremism, but it can never fully protect us from the type of terrorist assaults that have taken place over the past decade. Ideologies must be countered with ideas, and ideologies steeped in religion need to be challenged on religious grounds.

These days, in almost any foreign policy situation, ignoring the motivating influence of religious faith is a sure recipe for failure. Because so many terrorists, like those that struck the United States on 9/11, derive their legitimacy from extremist interpretations of their religion, the most effective counter is to empower the more tolerant, mainstream beliefs of that religion, especially among those communities most at risk of succumbing to violent propaganda. Although radical Islam is at the forefront of most religious conversations today, the lessons to be learned from combating extremism in an Islamic context apply equally well to any conflict having a religious dimension to it.

At latest count, some 86 percent of the world's seven billion inhabitants identify themselves as members of a religious community.[1] It may be fair to say that it is in the nature of things that humans instinctively aspire to a higher order of things. To ignore the motivating influence of religious ideas and not have a sympathetic understanding of those who identify strongly with the dictates of their faith would be to handicap ourselves severely in dealing with today's geopolitical realities. Religious political parties are becoming increasingly influential in North Africa and the Middle East in the wake of the Arab Spring, other conflicts in the region, and the current political evolution in Turkey. Muslims have been migrating to the West in large numbers, reshaping public attitudes and government policies in the process. This suggests that any effective long-term strategy to counter extremism should seek to capitalize on religion's extensive reach as well as its ethical values.

By the same token, it is important not to overgeneralize in ascribing religious motives to all extremist activities. Terrorism has long been used by people of various cultures for various reasons, primarily to achieve political aims. More than 95 percent of all known cases of suicide bombings between 1980 and 2004 had clear political objectives.[2] Whether in Chechnya or Sri Lanka, Kashmir or Gaza, the goals were always political and, more often than not, related to expelling an occupying force.[3]

It is also the case that those who committed these bombings came from diverse ethnic and religious backgrounds. Between 1982 and 1986, Hezbollah carried out forty-one suicide attacks against Israeli, American and French targets in Lebanon. Of these, only eight were carried out by Islamic extremists, twenty-seven by members of secular leftist political groups such as the Lebanese Communist Party, and three by Christians. All those involved were born in Lebanon and adhered to diverse, if not totally divergent, ideologies.[4] More recently, the anarchy and bloodshed that ensued in Iraq following the U.S. invasion was motivated by political competition between the Shiite and Sunni militias in a bid for power.

Thus the overriding motivation in most long-term, large-scale terrorist activities is political rather than religious. Where strong political passions exist, anyone can be a terrorist. Regardless of the cause, though, religion

1. Pearson Higher Education, "Religion."
2. Pape, *Dying to Win*.
3. Ibid.
4. Ibid., 14.

can sometimes offer a powerful antidote, if properly engaged. All of the major world religions share core tenets about neighborly concern and the betterment of humanity, tenets that can and often have been used to bridge differences between adversaries. In the case of Islamic extremism, however, the first challenge becomes that of empowering mainstream Muslims, most of whom despise terrorism. In the context of the Arab Spring, the West has a unique opportunity to do exactly this, if we are able to seize the moment.

GOVERNMENT EMPOWERMENT

Not long ago I had the opportunity to meet in Switzerland with a group of Tunisians and Egyptians to discuss their respective transitions to democracy. In response to one Egyptian participant, who said he and his colleagues had concluded that establishing one house of parliament would be less complicated and therefore preferable to establishing two, I said, "Don't you dare. Democracy is hard work and you need to build in as many checks and balances as you can from the outset. Otherwise, oppression will eventually creep back in, and you will begin to backslide, as some Eastern European states have in the past." I further observed, "Above all, you need to establish strong civilian control of the military. And if you need a good model for doing so, I suggest you take a hard look at the United States. The way we are structured, it is inconceivable that serious consideration could ever be given to a military takeover of the government." Little did I realize how prophetic that recommendation would prove to be in Egypt's transition.

After meeting with members of the Freedom and Justice Party, the political party of the Muslim Brotherhood in Egypt, John Kerry, then Chairman of the Senate Committee on Foreign Relations, commented, "You're certainly going to have to figure out how to deal with democratic governments that don't espouse every policy or value that you have." He added, "They certainly expressed a direction that shouldn't be a challenge to us, provided they follow through."[5] A short while later, William Hague, Britain's Foreign Minister, reflecting on the election victories of political Islamist groups in the Middle East, said this: "The test now is how they perform in office, of course, and we should not be afraid of talking to and working with those parties. We found already with the new Tunisian government, that they are very willing to work with us, that they agree with

---

5. David D. Kirkpatrick and Steven Lee Myers, "Overtures to Egypt's Islamists Reverse Longtime U.S. Policy," *New York Times,* January 3, 2012.

us about many global and regional issues, so I think we should be positive about that and not prejudge them."[6] Change of the magnitude that is currently taking place calls for determination and the courage to engage. The stakes are simply too high to let extremism take hold by default.

DOMESTIC CHALLENGES

A number of European countries have greater problems with their Muslim populations than we do in the United States. Many Muslims in Europe feel excluded and harassed by their governments. As pointed out in another *New York Times* piece in 2012, many Muslims in Europe feel excluded and harassed by their governments:

> The recognition and accommodation of Islamic religious practices, from clothing to language to education, does not mean capitulation to fundamentalism. On the contrary, only by strengthening the democratic rights of Muslim citizens to form associations, join political parties and engage in other aspects of civic life can Europe integrate immigrants and give full meaning to the abstract promise of religious liberty . . . It is Islam's absence in the institutions young European Muslims encounter, starting with the school's calendar, classroom and canteen, that contributes to anger and alienation.[7]

Engaging Muslim leaders as partners is one approach that is already bearing fruit in Britain, where authorities assert that Islamic leaders have been instrumental in helping to de-radicalize youth across the country.[8] Yet another fruitful approach for addressing such problems is the "Interfaith and Community Service Campus Challenge" issued by President Obama in March 2011, which challenges colleges and universities to sponsor a year of "interfaith service." As explained on the associated website,

> Interfaith service involves people from different religious and non-religious backgrounds tackling community challenges together—for example, Protestants and Catholics, Hindus and Jews, and Muslims and non-believers—building a Habitat for Humanity house together. Interfaith service impacts specific community

6. "William Hague: UN has failed on Syria."

7. Jonathan Laurence, "How to Integrate Europe's Muslims," *New York Times,* January 23, 2012.

8. Leiken and Brooke, "The Moderate Muslim Brotherhood."

challenges, from homelessness to mentoring to the environment, while building social capital and civility.[9]

A number of colleges and universities have answered this call.[10] Interfaith cooperation is also a highly effective means for cultivating moderate thinking.

In a 2010 article published in the *Christian Science Monitor*,[11] Hedieh Mirahmadi, President of the World Organization for Resource Development and Education (WORDE), and Mehreen Farooq, a Research Fellow at WORDE, presented a set of recommendations for curbing radicalization and extremism in the United States. They begin by noting that domestic radicalization is a problem and suggesting that "our domestic counterterrorism strategies end up alienating or underutilizing our best asset—the Muslim community." They advocate empowering moderate Muslims through education, research, and dialogue, contending that "Muslim scholars and community leaders are best suited to confront this problem by providing religious education (and re-education) to youth in both an authentic and 'cool' paradigm."[12]

One such Muslim scholar is Professor Abdullahi Ahmed an-Naim at Emory University in Atlanta, who has written widely on the relationship between Islam and government. He interprets the Qur'an as instructing Muslims to observe Sharia as their life's work, their responsibility, their struggle—not their government's. He even questions the concept of an Islamic state, viewing it as a post-colonial construct based on a mid-twentieth-century European-style state. As he explains, "My motivation is in fact about being an honest, true-to-myself Muslim, rather than someone complying with state dictates." Accordingly, he believes that the right answer for Muslims is a secular state that promotes human rights, so that both they and others can practice their faith freely. Branded as a heretic (a label he wears with some pride), Naim is attracting a notable following among young Muslims in Malaysia and Indonesia.[13]

---

9. The White House, "The President's Interfaith and Community Service Campus Challenge."

10. Allen, "Colleges, universities, pledge to interfaith community service."

11. Heideh Mirahmadi and Mehreen Farooq, "How to Fight Jihad in America," *Christian Science Monitor*, December 16, 2010.

12. Ibid.

13. Lampman, "Muslim reformer's 'heresy.'"

NGO/CIVIL SOCIETY EMPOWERMENT

While governments have considerable resources at their disposal to empower selected groups and individuals, NGOs enjoy greater freedom of movement, unencumbered as they are by any political agenda. They are also able to interact with populations in places that are sometimes inaccessible to governments, bring to bear an intimate knowledge of the areas in which they work, and capitalize on long-held relationships with the local communities. NGOs are thus uniquely equipped to help empower mainstream Muslims both domestically and internationally.

International

The international potential of NGOs was illustrated at a recent U.S. Institute of Peace event on "Pakistani Peacemakers: The Challenges for Civil Society Actors." While the substance focused on Pakistan, certain overarching principles emerged. As one commentator noted,[14] the empowerment of "traditional Muslim networks" can cultivate social cohesion and prevent the proliferation of extremism. She explained that these civil society networks are effective in promoting peace, since they are mindful of the religious rhetoric used by extremists and know how to counter it. In Pakistan, extremists often target Muslims who follow interpretations of Islam that run counter to their own. NGOs can and do speak out in the media against such attacks, often providing sounder interpretations of religious texts and principles in the process.

One of the more direct ways of empowering mainstream Islam is the approach that our own NGO, the International Center for Religion and Diplomacy (ICRD), has been taking in Pakistan. For the past eight years, we have been working with leaders of the religious schools (madrasas) to expand their curriculums to include the physical and social sciences, with a strong emphasis on religious tolerance and human rights, and to transform their pedagogy to promote critical thinking skills among the students. To date, we have engaged some 2,700 madrasa leaders from 1,611 madrasas, most of them located in the more radical areas of the country.

Experience has shown that once you are able to work your way past the veneer of hostility and rage and engage these madrasa leaders, not only do

14. Mehreen Farooq, Research Fellow at the World Organization for Resource Development.

they "get it," but many become ardent champions of the suggested change, often at great personal risk to themselves. Because this work is dealing with the ideas behind the guns, it is every bit as strategic as anything else that is taking place, either on or off the battlefield. Bombs typically create additional terrorists by exacerbating the cycle of revenge. Education, on the other hand, both drains the swamp of extremism and provides a better future for the children of Pakistan (and, indirectly, our own as well).

Domestic Opportunities in the U.S.

Domestically, NGOs can promote community-based initiatives centered on education, dialogue, and cooperation. Such efforts encourage and endorse activities that empower those in favor of dialogue over disruption, conversation over conflict. One such NGO that does this is Interfaith Works in Montgomery, Maryland, whose mission is to "pursue social justice with an emphasis on identifying and meeting the needs of the poor by leading and engaging Montgomery County's faith communities in service, education, and advocacy."[15] Interfaith Youth Core, founded in 2002 by Eboo Patel, promotes interfaith community service among university-aged students across the United States.[16]

NGOs such as these, as well as religious organizations that promote interfaith dialogue, form a family of organizations that advance moderate ideas. Still other organizations facilitate this same kind of understanding and cooperation on a broader scale. The Alliance for Peacebuilding, for example, provides a support base for the activities of the more than sixty organizations that operate under its umbrella. Soliya, one of its members, encourages students in the United States and across the Middle East to use technology to communicate with and learn from one another.[17] Extremists try to dominate discourse, while projects such as these work in the opposite direction.

In 2006, our center partnered with the International Institute of Islamic Thought (IIIT) and the Institute for Defense Analysis (IDA), the Pentagon's leading think tank, to convene a conference that brought thirty U.S. government officials together with a like number of American Muslim leaders to discuss how both groups could begin working together for

15. Interfaith Works, "History and Mission."
16. Interfaith Youth Core, "About IFYC."
17. Luce, "Muslims & Non-Muslims Hear About Terrorist Threat."

the common good. The catalyst for this conference was our recognition that the greatest strategic asset the United States has at its disposal in its global contest with militant Islam is the American Muslim community. Not only was this not being recognized, but we were unwittingly alienating this community through counterproductive overreactions to the events of 9/11. Incidents such as those in which Muslims have been pulled from planes for praying underscore the need for increased religious sensitivity in the execution of government policies.

One of the objectives of both that conference and a second follow-up conference a year later was determining the most effective way to inform U.S. foreign policy and public diplomacy with a Muslim perspective (in order to minimize the possibility of unintended consequences). In response to that challenge, we established a monthly Policy Forum that brings key congressional and executive branch staff together with respected leaders from the Muslim community to discuss issues that affect U.S. relations with Muslim countries overseas. The purpose of these forums is to provide the Washington policymaking community with a more nuanced understanding of Islam. From all indications, they appear to be achieving their intended goal. The forums also provide an excellent example of the synergy that can be achieved in empowering moderation when NGOs and government work together.

CONCLUSION

The question—How can the West empower mainstream Islam?—is broad and in some ways controversial. This attempt to provide a range of answers is by no means exhaustive; the possibilities are limited solely by our imaginations. The matter clearly deserves all the attention we can give it. As indicated earlier, the stakes are too high to do anything less.

9 Christian-Muslim Conflict Zones and Possibilities for Peace

David W. Shenk

Not long ago I received a letter from The Most Rev. Dr. Mouneer Hanna Anis, Bishop of the Episcopal /Anglican Diocese of Egypt. He wrote:

> Greetings in the Name of our Lord Jesus Christ! Today I attended an "iftar" or "breaking the fast" of Ramadan with the President of Egypt, the Prime Minister, and the Grand Imam of Al Azhar. I gave copies of your book, *A Muslim & Christian in Dialogue*, to the President and the Prime Minister (I had given a copy to the Grand Imam long ago) and they received them with great appreciation. I am grateful to God for this opportunity.
>
> May the Lord bless you!
>
> Bishop Mouneer[1]

Building Understanding

Most often, peace-building between Muslims and Christians develops in incremental steps of trust-building. The Bishop's letter refers to one such step: creating understanding between the church and the president of Egypt,

1. Letter of Bishop Mouneer Anis to David Shenk.

who is a member of the Muslim Brotherhood. The book he is referring to is a dialogue between myself and a Muslim theologian, Badru Kataregga. In that book Badru shares his faith with me, and I respond briefly chapter by chapter as an evangelical Christian. Then in twelve chapters I present the Christian faith while he responds.[2]

In regards to the event in Egypt, my modest involvement began a couple years earlier as a consequence of a letter entitled, "A Common Word Between Us and You."[3] This was a substantive letter developed by 138 Muslim scholars from around the world. Prince Ghazi bin Muhammad was the principal architect of the letter. It was released in October 2007, addressed to all Christian leaders. The letter observes that Christians and Muslims comprise half the world's population and both movements claim to be heirs of the faith of Abraham. That faith is a mandate to fear and love God and to love one's neighbor. Therefore, both the Muslim ummah and the Christian church carry special responsibility for enhancing the peace of the world.

That letter was released six years ago. The response has been immensely varied, from both Muslim and Christian communities. There has been sharp critique as well as enthusiastic affirmation. One of many responses came at the initiative of the Yale Divinity School Center for Faith and Culture, which convened a forum of two hundred Christian and Muslim leaders for a substantive theological dialogue. I was privileged to participate.

At that forum, I met representatives of Al Azhar University in Egypt. I had in hand the Kateregga–Shenk dialogue, and inquired whether Al Azhar would consider publishing the book as a contribution to inter-religious understanding. That was the beginning of a conversation of several years. The book is now in Arabic, endorsed by Al Azhar. It is this book that Bishop Mouneer was referring to. Hostility between Muslims and Christians is often grounded in misinformation. The purpose of the dialogue is very modest; it is about building understanding.

DEVELOPING TRUST

The commitment to build respectful understanding is absolutely essential to peacemaking. However, misunderstanding is not the only reason for conflict. The calling to peacemaking is multifaceted. Eliza Griswold demonstrates the urgency of varied approaches to peacemaking in *The Tenth*

2. Kateregga and Shenk, *A Muslim and a Christian in Dialogue*.

3. "A Common Word."

Parallel: Dispatches from the Fault Line between Christianity and Islam.[4] She invested seven years immersed within several African and Asian regions along the tenth parallel north that are conflict zones for Muslims and Christians: Nigeria, Sudan, Somalia, Indonesia, Malaysia, and the Philippines. She identified the missionary mandate within both the Muslim and Christian communities as one source of conflict. She also discovered political dynamics as a potential source of conflict. What she discovered is not a surprise.

When confrontational or even sensitive approaches to evangelism backfire, the inclination is often to simply avoid the call to witness. Some peacemaking in Nigeria is an example of that kind of avoidance in the interest of coexistence. Both Muslims and Christians have been wounded by sometimes violent reaction to both Muslim and Christian proselytizing. It is in this volatile context that Reverend Dr. James Mavel Wuye and Imam Dr. Muhammad Nurayan Ashafa have developed alternative peacemaking approaches. These former polemicists now travel the country meeting with Muslim and Christian audiences to urge building trust and friendships between the two communities. They model trust-building friendship.

The pastor and the imam tell me that they avoid theological discussions, for that would bring a wedge between them. That is one approach to peacemaking, avoiding discussion of theological differences. Nevertheless, these peacemakers travel Nigeria as a team, meeting both Muslim and Christian audiences, pleading for tolerance and respect. They do this while acknowledging that they are committed to bearing witness to their respective faiths and inviting others to believe. They have not muted their witness. They each believe that peacemaking must include space for the other to bear witness. Fundamentally this Nigerian team is simply cultivating the kinds of relations that create trust.

The imam and pastor might be more typical of Christian-Muslim relations than we assume. In order to explore the status of relations in the African setting, the Pew Forum on Religion and Public Life conducted a study of Christian–Muslim relations in nineteen sub-Saharan African nations. This 2010 survey would support the observation that the fraternal tolerance Imam Muhammad and Reverend James model is normative for Christian-Muslim relations in the countries they surveyed. Not only were relations cordial, but both the Muslim and Christian communities benefited from cordial relations by attracting growing numbers of adherents.

4. Griswold, *Tenth Parallel.*

Cordiality and witness were complementary. The study observes that where there is hostility, neither community benefits and both Muslims and Christians suffer.[5]

Theological Dialogue

In contrast to the gingerly approach to theology that the imam and pastor model, theology is quite prominent in dialogues that I and other Anabaptists have been engaged in within Iran. These Iranian Shi'ite theologians assert that theology is at the heart of the Iranian conflict with the Western powers and the conflict with Sunni Muslim communities. For that reason they request that the dialogues we are engaged in be grounded in theological encounter, an encounter that respects the commitment of both communities to faithful witness to their respective faiths. They believe that when political systems are at an impasse, theological leadership has a special responsibility to seek a way forward.

The beginning of these dialogical encounters was when Anabaptist churches in North America sent material aid to Iran following an earthquake in 1989. In time that humanitarian response opened possibilities for authentic conversations about the faith foundations of these respective communities.

Consequently for the last ten years Iranian Shi'ite–North American Anabaptist theological dialogues have happened about every two years. They alternate between North America and Iran. The next event will focus on ethical foundations. Scholars from both sides make presentations for discussion and response; the papers are then published for distribution beyond the dozen or so scholars who participate. One fruit of these dialogues is that several of us were guests of honor at the twenty-fifth anniversary of the Iranian revolution. The audience of hundreds of thousands thunderously denounced the U.S.A.; yet we were embraced. A couple times I was addressed as "dear brother David." We asked the reason for this reception. Our hosts responded that they knew we represented the church, not the agendas of the Western powers.

It is essential that such dialogues not bypass the indigenous churches. For that reason I have made a point of meeting church leaders when we convene in Iran for these dialogues. Church leaders have been most supportive of these efforts; one comment was that such dialogues help to provide

5. Pew Forum, "Tolerance and Tension."

credibility and space for the church. The churches in Iran have faced special challenges, and we are grateful for opportunities to be encouragers.

BEARING WITNESS TO THE PEACE OF JESUS

Annually, Iranian Shi'ites have a Mahdi conference, where several thousand clergy gather to contemplate the coming reign of the Mahdi. They believe he will complete the political expansion of Islam into all the world that Muhammad began in Medina fourteen centuries ago. In line with that vision, they believe the Mahdi will appear with Jesus and together they will extend the political and spiritual reach of Islam throughout the world.

On one occasion I was among several Christian invitees to make a presentation at the Mahdi Conference. I chose to speak on the peace of Christ. I had the privilege of meeting the President of Iran as well as addressing a couple thousand clerics. There were six Christians present. When the assembly dismissed for the late morning prayers, we Christians met in a prayer circle, interceding for the empowerment of the Holy Spirit and for the revelation of grace upon all the assembled clerics.

Then I was invited to take the podium. I invited the clerics to send greetings to the churches that I visit around the world by waving their hands. I was amazed seeing hundreds of turbaned clerics sending greetings to the churches.

In my twenty-minute message, I briefly reviewed the Jesus narrative: the prophetic expectation, his virgin birth, his Nazareth inaugural sermon proclaiming good news, his ethical teaching in the Sermon on the Mount, his refusal to accept the military or political option for establishing the kingdom of God, his colt ride into Jerusalem as a fulfillment of Zechariah's prophecy that the colt-riding Messiah would proclaim a kingdom of peace to all nations that would do away with all weapons of war, his cleansing of the temple with an army of singing children, his washing the feet of the betrayer at the last supper, his rebuke to Peter who sought to defend Jesus with the sword when soldiers appeared to arrest him, his cry of forgiveness and invitation to reconciliation as he died on the cross with outstretched arms, his resurrection commission to the disciples to carry forward his mission to all nations. When I concluded, the moderator exclaimed, "We did not know this about Jesus. We must investigate. And you Christians need to provide us with the necessary books to explore what you have shared today."

Peacemaking in the Political Arena

After the Mahdi Conference, I and a colleague requested a meeting with U.S. State Department officials to appeal for the U.S. Government to enter into dialogue with the Iranian authorities. We had a most energetic conversation. They were astonished that the door is open for substantive theological dialogue with Iranian Shi'ites. Our plea was to be in dialogue rather than fight. As we left, one of the officers said, "You have been heard!" Significantly the day of our visit we were invited to a forum at the State Department on engaging militant Muslims theologically rather than militarily. We were grateful that such conversations were happening. Surely the church has a special role in times when the political systems are at an impasse.

Shortly before entering this open door in Tehran, the small evangelical community in Kosovo had invited me to participate in a public dialogue on peacemaking. That was an amazing invitation, for Kosovo has been through the fires of Christian-Muslim conflict, wherein Christians planted crosses in the ashes of burned Muslim villages. The inviting community bathed the plans in prayer as they encountered numerous obstacles. Finally in faith they rented the largest hall in Kosovo. It packed out with six hundred present from across the country. Most of the key Muslim and Christian leaders were present. I spoke simply about Jesus crucified and risen. Jesus goes to the root causes of conflict. In his life, crucifixion, and resurrection he offers the grace of forgiveness and reconciliation between us and God and with one another.

My Muslim dialogue companion was astonished. He was intrigued by the forgiveness and reconciliation of Christ. We also explored the role of justice in reconciliation. With support from the Qur'an he insisted that justice must be the precursor to peace. That event helped to open the door for further conversations between key Muslim and Christian leaders on the role of the small evangelical church in helping to minister healing to the grievous wounds of the Kosovo conflict.

On a subsequent trip the evangelical leadership and I were invited to meet with the Islamic Department of the Kosovo University. The assigned theme was truth and freedom. Students and faculty were present, as were the key writers of the Kosovo constitution. I am told that the presentation created considerable foment. I centered the plea for religious freedom solidly within biblical revelation: we are created in God's image; God gives us freedom to choose; we need to love our neighbor; no government has the authority to rob us of the freedom that God has bestowed upon us. Of course our Muslim hosts recognized that a case can be made for freedom of choice from within the Qur'an and Islamic traditions. We applaud any steps in the directions of enhancing such freedoms. It seems that we were heard! The constitution as it now stands does indeed provide remarkable provision for religious freedom.

FOUNDATIONS FOR PEACEMAKING

Christ-centered peacemaking refuses to be distracted by the fractures between Muslims and Christians or by opposition, whether that objection comes from fellow Christians or zealous Muslims. In the examples of peacemaking described above, several principles emerge that are essential to a Christian approach to effective peacemaking.

1. Be both bold and gentle ambassadors of Jesus the prince of peace.

2. Recognize the yearnings for peace within everyone. The Christian peacemaker nurtures any inclinations toward peacemaking that are present either in the Muslim or Christian communities.

3. Confess that Jesus is the ultimate peacemaker. It is Jesus who astounded the throngs by commanding, "Love your enemy!"

4. Pursue peace. Doors do not open automatically. We knock on doors until they open.

5. Do acts of loving kindness. Normally it is good deeds that open the door for peacemaking.

6. Be patient. The seeds of peace are mostly unobtrusive, even unnoticed, "mustard seeds" that flourish in time.

7. Encounter the enormous obstacles with the empowerment of the Holy Spirit. Peacemaking is bathed in prayer.

8. Be committed to the church. The faithful church is an authentic peacemaking community; it is only in the church that the reconciliation and forgiveness of Christ are known.

9. Be ambassadors of Christ and his kingdom, not ambassadors of a particular political or national system.

10. Be "salt" within the political systems. Christians seek to influence society or political systems with the principles of peacemaking. The

witness by the church is that the gospel of peace is revealed in the Man on the cross who forgives his enemies. This Jesus is healing grace for the person and for the nations.

CONFLICT TRANSFORMATION

I conclude with another account of peacemaking that weaves these strands together. In 1998, the town of Solo in central Java (Indonesia) had experienced violent clashes between ethnic and religious groups. A joint Muslim–Christian commission formed to work on peacemaking. A youthful and jovial pastor was selected to give leadership to this impossible task of peacemaking in a city infected with anger.

As one step they decided to translate and publish the dialogue that Bishop Mouneer wrote about. Then they invited Christian guests from abroad to come for the official launching of the book. First we met with a congenial gathering of eighty peace-loving Muslims and Christians. After my presentation there was a question from the back of the room. "You are a man of peace, but our impression is that American Christians are terrorists."

With permission from the chair, I responded. "I am not here as a representative of the U.S. nor can I represent the enormous diversity among American Christians. We cry out to God for forgiveness for the times our nation has betrayed the way of peace among the nations. However, I am here as an ambassador of Jesus Christ and his kingdom. That kingdom is founded upon the suffering redemptive love revealed in Jesus crucified and risen. His kingdom is healing for the nations and is our only eternal hope for reconciliation between every tribe and nation. Before the recent wars began, I joined with several thousand other Christians in signing a letter to our President imploring him to desist from going to war. We were not heard; however, we did try to call for another way."

That response was aired on national television. I am told that even jihadists expressed appreciation for this witness to the peace of Christ that transcends national identities and that challenges the nations to cultivate peaceful discourse.

We were then taken to the Indonesian Hizbullah command center. The officers were armed and dressed in military uniform. This center had 10,000 militia, had burned churches, and they were known for attacking Christian leaders. We sat in a circle, about forty Christians and forty

Muslims. They explained that their mission was to fight to defend Islam and kill their enemies. We commented that Jesus shows another way, that of love for the enemy. They were astonished. However, I sometimes experience similar astonishment when addressing Christian audiences in North America.

Then the pastor who had organized this meeting handed the commander a copy of the just published dialogue. He paged through it, and then shed tears. He said he was weeping because this book was revealing another way, of respect for others, even if one disagrees. He ordered fifty copies for all his officers. We then had a grand feast together prepared for the Christian guests by the Hizbullah.

I asked the pastor how this transformation had come about. He told of his first visit to the Hizbullah commander's home, and experiencing rebuff as the commander exclaimed, "You are an infidel and I can kill you! What do you want?"

The pastor responded, "I want to drink tea with you."

For the next couple years this youthful pastor had a cup of tea with the commander regularly. Then the pastors in Solo invited the Hizbullah officers to accompany them in a chartered plane for a joint reconstruction team in Banda Aceh where the tsunami had hit. The commander slept in the same room with the pastor; they became friends. Nowadays the Hizbullah commander has become an advocate for the church and works with the Christian leaders in quenching fires that threaten the peace between Muslims and Christians.

CONCLUSION: LOTS OF TEA

I asked the pastor, "How do you account for this transformation?"

With a burst of laughter he responded, "Lots of cups of tea!" Then he added, "This is the work of the Holy Spirit. We move forward prayerfully for it is only through the empowerment of the Holy Spirit that our witness to the peace of Christ can be heard."

May God raise up hundreds and thousands of young people, who like the young pastor in Solo, press forward as peacemakers in our tumultuous world, bearing witness to the crucified Man from Nazareth in whom we are reconciled to God and to one another. That calling requires the hospitable fellowship of drinking lots of tea together.[6]

6. Shenk, "Gospel of Reconciliation within the Wrath of Nations."

10 How Personal Forgiveness Created a Platform for Global Peacemaking

LISA R. GIBSON

FOUR DAYS BEFORE CHRISTMAS, a twenty-year-old army specialist packed the last of his belongings into a medium-sized suitcase before catching a taxi to the airport in Berlin, Germany. It was an exciting day for him; having been away serving his country for nearly two years, he was heading home to spend Christmas with his family in Michigan. It was to be a long series of flights—first to Frankfurt, then to London Heathrow, and then on to New York City before finally arriving in Detroit.

On December 21, 1988, this man's flight landed at London Heathrow Airport to refuel. The earlier flight had been overbooked, and he was bumped to the later flight. The plane was only half full, so he was looking forward to having some extra room to sleep on the overnight flight to the United States. He boarded the plane with the other passengers and settled into his seat, beaming with anticipation. As he looked out the window at the ground crew going about their business, a suitcase was being loaded onto the plane that was different from all the others.

The head purser made the announcement over the intercom with the final departure instructions. "Ladies and gentlemen, I would like to thank you for flying with us today on this seven-hour flight to New York. The last of the luggage is being loaded on to the plane. In a few moments, we will be ready to pull away from the gate. Please take your seats, and be sure your seat belts are securely fastened and your seats are in the upright position. This is Pan Am Flight one-oh-three."

The plane pulled back from the gate, taxied down the runway, and revved its engines as it began to lift off from the ground and into the horizon. The young man looked at the ground one last time as it slowly became more and more distant and thought, "This will be the last takeoff before I once again plant my feet firmly on the ground in the United States."

At 1900 hours local time, the last communications were heard from the plane. It was at that time that my brother's life became a memory.

In 1988, my brother Ken was killed in the terrorist bombing of Pan Am Flight 103 over Lockerbie, Scotland. Ken was twenty years old at the time and was serving in the army in Berlin, Germany. The whole family was excited to see him since he had been away serving our country in the army for nearly two years.

I was only eighteen years old when my brother Ken was killed. Too young to have learned to deal with the kind of loss I was facing, yet too old to deny the magnitude. I had just finished the first term of my freshman year at college. It was a time that should have been filled with fun, adventure, and hope for the future. Instead, my life was turned upside down in a matter of minutes. My older brother was taken from me and my family in one of the most hateful and political type of losses. I have always thought that had he died in a car accident or by natural causes, it may have been easier. But the motivation behind this act, intentionally targeting innocent people traveling by commercial airliner, was unspeakable.

My brother was one of 270 people killed on that fateful day. It was a plane full of young people with the average age around twenty-four. Many were making their way home for the holidays to celebrate with loved ones. Since the tragedy happened over Christmas break I had a little time to work through things with my family. A time that should have been dedicated to Christmas festivities, spending time with family and opening gifts, was instead consumed by grief, confusion, and bombardment by the media. All of a sudden, the quiet no-nonsense existence we had lived was now being exposed to the public eye. I learned very quickly the power of media in communicating messages to the world. As Christians, we represented not only ourselves, but Christians everywhere. Though only eighteen years of age, I knew that I reflected Jesus Christ in the way I responded. I wanted to honor him and respond the way the Bible called me to respond. The problem was I wasn't feeling anything at the time. I was simply numb and in denial of the reality of it all. I had gone into survival mode after hearing the news. It was like living a dream, rather a nightmare. A nightmare that I had convinced myself I might just be able to overcome if I just kept moving forward. So, as soon as Christmas break ended, I returned to school. Since we didn't have any indication of when my brother's body would be returned, I convinced myself that throwing myself into school work was the most effective way to move forward. After all, what good was I doing just sitting at home feeling sad? There were no answers, just lots of questions. They were questions that I would later learn we would continue to ask for the next twenty years.

Any idea I had of moving beyond the tragedy came to a screeching halt when I arrived back at college to find the Pan Am 103 terrorist attack to be the talk of the campus. In hindsight, I can see that was appropriate. It was, after all, the worst terrorist attack against Americans at the time. Prior to this tragedy, most terrorist attacks involved hijacking planes and demanding ransoms for kidnapped people. This was an international incident that just happened to impact my life directly. It was a private nightmare that I was desperately trying to escape while everyone in the world wanted to talk about it. I was walking around in a haze while alternating between sadness and disbelief, hoping that my brother Ken was alive somewhere safe.

My first encounter with the reality of what the next twenty-three years would hold happened when I sat in my political science class and I listened as my Muslim professor from Iran stood up and condoned the acts. At the time the media was communicating that they believed the bombing to be in retaliation for the U.S. accidentally shooting down an Iranian passenger plane. So from my professor's worldview it was an eye for an eye. When I heard him make those statements to the class, it snapped me out of my denial and I began to boil inside. I could not believe what I was hearing. Did he just say what I think he said? How could someone believe this? I wanted to say something, but I was afraid of what would come out of my mouth if I spoke. So, I just got up and walked out. I went back to my dorm room, sat alone, and wept. It was the first substantial cry I had experienced since hearing the news. The false world of security I had been living in was beginning to unravel.

Several days later I sat down with that professor and shared that I lost my brother in the Lockerbie bombing, and he apologized. Of course, he had no idea that I had been personally affected, or he would not have said what he had. He wasn't a completely insensitive man as I had thought him to be. Before hearing about my personal connection, it was just an international incident that was highly relevant to my international political science class. Then it became more, much more.

Our conversation transitioned from my personal loss to my quest for answers. It was a quest that would continue through the better part of my remaining three years in college. I set my sights on trying to find answers, believing if I could understand the "why" behind terrorism, maybe I could prevent future acts. I was a political science major in college and even went on to do my senior thesis on Middle East terrorism with that same Iranian professor advising me on my project. My question was what could possibly compel someone to blow up a plane full of innocent people? I learned the ins and outs of Islamic terrorism and compared that to other acts of terrorism throughout history. I concluded that at the heart of terrorism is hate and the reason terrorists attack innocent people is to create fear and chaos. In the end, even though I could articulate and discuss the topic, it left me with more questions.

It was one of those times in my life where I just sat there with God and said, "Okay, God, I get it, now what?"

God clearly spoke to my heart. "Lisa, we live in a fallen world, and the only answer is Jesus Christ."

The question that God placed in my heart, after all the dust settled, was simply this: "How might I be a part of seeing this tragedy redeemed and see some good come out of it?"

Prior to September 11, 2001, Lockerbie was the single biggest attack on innocent American citizens. Long before the events that made "War on Terror" household words, my family and I had been actively engaged in the war on terrorism. Those words were firmly embedded in my consciousness. Little did I know at the time, but those words would determine my life course for the next twenty-four years. Now, after more than two decades, I know what it is to wage the battle in the physical and the spiritual realms.

After a lengthy investigation, a Libyan intelligence agent was convicted. After years of the U.S. government persistently pursuing justice, Libya accepted responsibility and paid civil damages to the families.

While the victims' family members were actively at work on the geopolitical level, God was also at work within me on a personal level. For years I was simply indifferent. I didn't know any Muslims and that was the way I wanted to keep it. As a Christian, I knew it was wrong to hate and that I was called to forgive. But as I read the Bible, I was challenged because I learned it was more than not hating my enemy—it was about loving them. At the heart of terrorism is hate and fear. The only way to effectively fight the battle is to walk in the opposite spirit. Too many Christians are trying to fight the battle with the enemy's weapons. Where there is hate, we must respond in love. Where there is fear, we must respond in faith.

There are three verses that commanded me to love my enemies. Luke 6:27–28 (NRSV) says: "But I say to you that listen, Love your enemies, do good to those who hate you, bless those who curse you, pray for those who abuse you." It goes on in verse 32 to say: "If you love those who love you, what benefit is that to you?" Romans 12:21 further confirms this with the message to overcome evil with good.

So I made a choice. It was a choice that few people understood, and no one would have faulted me if I had not decided to make it. It was a choice most exemplified in this quote by M. Scott Peck: "The whole course of human history may depend on a change of heart in one solitary and even humble individual—for it is in the solitary mind and soul of the individual that the battle between good and evil is waged and ultimately won or lost."[1]

I made the choice to take the road less traveled; rather than succumbing to bitterness or simple indifference, I chose to respond in love. With the realization that love is an action, I began to look for opportunities to reach out in love to my enemies.

My first step was to send a letter of forgiveness to the man convicted of the bombing. The emotions were still pretty fresh for me. Would he even get the letter? And if he did, how would he respond?

Even as I sat down to write the letter, I wasn't completely feeling the forgiveness in my heart. Frankly, it was simply an act of obedience. The Bible said that I was to forgive and love my enemies, and I was attempting to do that in the most concrete way I knew how. So I sat down with a pen and paper in hand and prepared to write. I asked myself, "What do I say exactly? The guy is going to think I am crazy. Why even bother? Will he even be able to understand it?" All these were the doubts that ran through my head.

After wrestling for what seemed like an hour, I felt free to begin to write. Since I couldn't speak or write Arabic, I had no choice but to write in English.

"Dear Mr. Megrahi . . ."

1. Peck, *www.BrainyQuote.com*.

I simply introduced myself and told him my brother was killed on the Lockerbie plane, Pan Am Flight 103.

"Only God really knows if you are responsible for this act," I said. "But as a Christian, I need to forgive you."

It may have been one of the shortest and simplest letters I had ever written, but it was done. I sealed the envelope and addressed it to the prison in Glasgow. As I drove to the post office, I continued in deep thought. What effect would this really have?

"I would like one airmail stamp to Scotland, please," I told the postal clerk.

I affixed the stamp on the envelope firmly, then held it one last time before handing it over to the clerk to be mailed. As I walked away, I looked up to heaven and said with a sigh, "Okay, God, I did what you asked. May your purposes be fulfilled."

I never would have expected my letter would get to him. I assumed that if it did get to him, it would end up in the trash. Despite my doubts, the letter was delivered to him. Not only did he get the letter, but he actually responded to it in early July 2004. I will never forget sitting in silence on the living room couch of my apartment, just me, God, and the letter—a letter from a terrorist in prison. I tried to allow myself to appreciate the magnitude of that. "I wonder what it says. God, I hope it doesn't say something mean, because I am not sure I could take that."

I did not want to open it. I was afraid. But I did open it. I was astonished at what it said. It was a very kind letter that expressed his condolences for my loss and shared verses from both the Koran and the Bible about how God answers prayer. He said he prayed I would be happy in my life and suffer no such sadness in the future.

Reading his letter validated my belief that forgiveness is a powerful instrument of God that does more than hate ever could to bring about change. Following the writing of my letter of forgiveness, I began to build a relationship with the new Libyan ambassador to the United States, and in January 2005, I made a personal reconciliation trip to Libya. I met with individual citizens and government officials, and in each case I simply told them my story: as a Christian I needed to go and get to know them so that I could forgive them and learn to love them.

As I would share my story, time and again, the walls would fall, and even grown men would weep and say, "I will do anything I can to help you." I started to realize that my trip was more about them than it was about me.

For the first time, I understood that there is power in walking out what it is to love our enemies that breaks something in the spiritual realm—it breaks the power of pride.

As the walls fell, God's grace flowed. I found myself asking questions like "What was it like to live in Libya?" and "What was it like when the U.S. bombed Tripoli in 1986?" The responses I received were honest and heartfelt: "It is so good for you to ask. No one has ever asked me that before." After hearing about their lives I came back to the U.S. inspired to do something to help improve their lives. Out of that experience, the Peace and Prosperity Alliance was birthed to provide humanitarian and education projects to serve the country of Libya.

On September 23, 2009, I engaged in the ultimate act of forgiveness and unconditional love when I met with and forgave Libyan leader Muammar Gaddafi, one of the world's most notorious terrorists and the man many believe was responsible for the Lockerbie bombing. It was a meeting that had been many years in the making, because as I look back, I couldn't have met with him any earlier. My heart wasn't ready. That day was the appointed time as was evidenced by my sense of complete peace and joy. That could only come from the work God had done in my heart. I had no fear and had a keen sense in the moment that I was experiencing one of the key assignments I had been put on this earth for.

It was a brief meeting, only about fifteen minutes total. Since I didn't know how much time I would have, I also gave him a card sharing the things I felt led to tell him. It was a Thomas Kinkade card, with one of those idyllic scenes of a log cabin in a majestic mountain setting. To me it exemplified peace. What I shared, both in person and in the card, was what Romans 12 calls us to do. I shared with him that I had forgiven, blessed him, told him about my efforts to serve the Libyan people, and even shared about how I had been praying for him daily. In the card I told him that I had bought a "Gaddafi watch" on my first trip to Libya and said, "Every day I look down at the watch, and I say a prayer for you."

Gaddafi's countenance was very stoic throughout the entire meeting until the end, when I gave him a gift. It was a simple gesture of attempting to do something good to him as the scripture says. Since I wanted it to have spiritual meaning but also be something he might actually use, I settled on a Cross pen. When I gave him the pen, I could tell he was touched. It was the only time he smiled, and he said, "Thank you." As his countenance softened, it was as if for a brief moment I saw his humanity and his heart.

God reminded me of the scripture he gave me for Gaddafi from Proverbs 14:12 (NRSV) that says, "There is a way that seems right to a person but its end is the way to death." I thought about who God had desired Gaddafi to be and how very far he had gone from that. That meeting was a culmination of many years of striving to see the country of Libya change. It was a long, hard journey that came to a close for me as I sat face-to-face with the man responsible for my brother's death. I told him my desire was to focus on reconciliation with Libya by building a bridge of friendship between the people of the United States and Libya through goodwill and service.

That night as I returned to my hotel, I found myself deep in thought. What did I actually accomplish there? I did not know for sure. But I sensed God was very pleased. I felt almost giddy inside. I thought to myself "no one will ever know this happened." There were no media crews. Just one single television camera for Libyan television. I figured if people did hear about it, it would be portrayed by Libyan television as something completely different than what actually happened. Little did I know the following evening, as I was flying back to Colorado, Muammar Gaddafi was sharing the story of the meeting on CNN in an interview with Fareed Zakaria. In that interview one of the most notorious terrorists and evil dictators shared how he was touched by our meeting.

The very next morning, I awoke to my phone ringing off the hook with calls from every major media outlet trying to ascertain if I was the woman who met with Gaddafi. They had gotten my name and contact information from the Libyan Ambassador. The other Lockerbie family members who they had called denied the story as a fabrication by Gaddafi. "No Lockerbie family member would meet with Gaddafi," some said.

They were wrong. One woman, on a mission from God, simply trying to love her enemies and overcome evil with good, had chosen to meet with Gaddafi. It was insanity to some and courageous to others. Perhaps it was just the insanity of grace. At a minimum, the path that I have taken is a revolutionary approach when compared with the other victims' family members, many of whom have chosen to focus on bitterness and revenge. As such, the story of our meeting went around the world and was covered by nearly every large media outlet. CNN was the first to share my provocative statement that "Love is the most effective weapon in the war on terror." Although there was criticism by some, the positive response far outweighed the negative. My email inbox was flooded with responses from people all over the world who thanked me and asked if there were ways they could help with my work. Many were Muslims and several were Libyans. I believe the response was so positive because when people see unconditional love in action, it is so compelling they are drawn to it. On that day, the message that was communicated to the world was simply this: Daily there is a battle being waged between the forces of good and evil through love and hate, but in the end love always wins.

The completion of the redemptive cycle of overcoming evil with good happened in June 27, 2011 as I spoke to a crowd of 100,000 people in Freedom Square in Benghazi, Libya, on the day the International Court issued the arrest warrant for Muammar Gaddafi. I had gone to Libya to deliver much-needed medical supplies during the revolution. After sharing my story with leaders of the revolution, they asked me to speak at the rally. I simply shared that I came there as a fellow victim of Gaddafi's terror to stand with them during their time of need. To let them know that they were not alone and that there were people all over the world praying for them.

For the first time in all my trips to Libya, I saw the pictures on the wall of martyrs of all the Libyan people who had disappeared or been killed by Muammar Gaddafi, and my heart broke for them. I poured out my heart to the people, sharing about my years of serving in Libya and desire to continue helping them, and they were clearly touched. At one point, they interrupted my speech and began chanting, "Thank you, Lisa!" in English. I was so humbled. I felt as though I was experiencing a key moment in history and realized how privileged I was to be a part of it. For the first time, I really understood what I would have missed if I hadn't chosen to follow God down this path.

As I walked through the massive crowd of people with our armored military escorts, I was met with smiles and people wanting to shake my hand and just say thank you. I felt like a rock star while all along thinking about how grateful I was for God allowing me to be a part of this. The incredibly emotional day ended with a former army general and his sons coming to the hotel just to meet me personally and present me with a special award certificate that was fresh off the press. It was one of the most honoring experiences I have ever had. I felt the most blessed I have in my lifetime. Although I went back to Libya to facilitate a leadership institute in January 2012, I knew in that moment that the circle of reconciliation came to a close on June 27, 2011.

Despite the ending of one chapter, the remainder of the book still remains to be written. Out of the tragedy, I have gained a platform for peacemaking around the world. I have shared my story of reconciliation with ambassadors from the Middle East at a luncheon in Washington, D.C., and shared the same story with persecuted Christians in the refugee camps of Khartoum, Sudan. The same story, God's story, has been shared time and again around the world. I have also developed a mediation practice and taught conflict resolution to leaders in Afghanistan, Iraq, Libya, Egypt, and countless other places.

As a result of my loss, I have had the privilege to minister God's healing touch of peace to many around the world. In January of 2012, I was facilitating a leadership institute in Benghazi, Libya, the seedbed of the revolution. We were teaching courses in leadership, ethics, project management, and conflict resolution. Our hope was to assist with rebuilding Libya by teaching classes that relate to a civil society. I had the privilege to teach conflict resolution. As always, as part of the course, I shared my own story and we discussed ways to help Libya to move toward reconciliation and peace. At the break, one of the doctors in the course came up to speak with me. She was a very bright woman who was prone to brashness, and I had already seen her offend some of her classmates in some of the exercises. As she approached me I could see she was not happy. But I was not deterred.

"I appreciate you sharing your story. But I want you to know I hate Gaddafi and I hate those people who supported him. And I see them walking through the halls of this hospital. But I know who they are and what they did to me and my family."

She went on to share about the ways her family had suffered under the Gaddafi regime. It was abhorrent and she was incredibly justified in being angry. But beyond what she was saying, I heard her heart. I validated the loss and the importance of grieving. I encouraged her that it would take time, but that this country needs strong leaders who can move the country forward. In order to do that, they must be able to forgive and reconcile.

"Do you believe God is the judge in Islam?" I asked.

"Yes, and Gaddafi is burning in hell," she said.

"Then why do you need to continue to carry this? As long as you continue to hold onto this, Gaddafi continues to control you from the grave." I said.

In that moment, that once brash woman immediately softened and began to cry. I reached out and gave her a hug. It was a tender moment that I will never forget. I realized that out of my personal loss, and willingness to respond in peace and love, that I had been given an incredible gift. I could speak into people's lives on the individual human level, and challenge the world on a global policy level. It is a unique and strategic place to be. But it was only because I had accepted the call of God to take the road less traveled. I had earned the blessing of influence and seeing God move miraculously because I had chosen the path of peace. This is what Jesus meant when he said, "Blessed are the peacemakers, for they will be called children of God" (Matt 5:9). If God had shown me the direction my journey was going to go, I would have likely shrunk back in fear. Instead, I simply followed in faith even when things didn't make sense. As I was faithful, God was even more faithful. Because of that my life truly has been blessed.

11 A Holy Land We Hold in Trust

SAMI AWAD

I AM GRATEFUL FOR the invitation to participate in this conversation. It is great to be a part of this historic school of evangelicals who have been working for so many years to get involved and be a catalyst for peace in the Holy Land and the Middle East. One of the longstanding questions about evangelicals used to be: What can we do to get them involved? I think now we can ask a different question. What do we do now that you are involved? I think we have reached the point where there are enough evangelicals—pastors, organizations, committed Christians—that we can truly make a difference.

I want to describe the work that I am engaging in, in Palestine, in Israel, in the Holy Land. My organization is called Holy Land Trust. I want to describe how our work has evolved over the last few years to focus more and more on what Jesus wants us to do, not on what we want to do. Because many times we have our agendas, we have our good intentions, we have our desires for peace. We like things to happen. We like to see conflict end, we like to see violence end. And of course, this is God's will in our lives. But Jesus wants us to move forward with his methods and means for making peace as well.

What is the language that he wants us to speak to those that are suffering? What is the language that he wants us to speak to those who are inflicting the suffering, as well? It's very easy for us to label them, to judge them, to even demonize and dehumanize those who cause suffering. It's a natural reaction to just look at them and demonize them for the violence that they commit. And we always need to ask the question: Is this the style of Jesus? Is this how Jesus would talk to the oppressor? And how he would talk to the oppressed?

Fourteen years ago, I started Holy Land Trust as an organization (www.holylandtrust.org). Our slogan is: "Strengthening communities for the future." People have asked me for years how we came up with the name Holy Land Trust and with the slogan, "strengthening communities for the future." And I always blame the board. This is what the board wanted and this is what they came up with. It wasn't until recently that I figured out why we have Holy Land Trust as a name and why we have "strengthening communities for the future" as a slogan.

Sometimes we want to be partners with Jesus in setting up his plans for us. We want to argue with him and negotiate with him about what should happen. But sometimes we should just accept things, and maybe it will take ten years after that to really understand what his intention was.

Now we feel we understand. Holy Land, this is what it is. It is the Holy Land. If you are a Muslim, or you are a Jew, or you are a Christian, one thing you claim for this land is that it is holy; it is sacred land. And we all believe this. This is where our Christ was born. This is where he walked. This is where the disciples walked, the prophets walked. So for all of the religions of that land, as much as they fight with each other and disagree with each other, one thing that they would agree on is the concept that this is holy, sacred land.

Trust—the word *trust* for us has two meanings. The first is the trusting relationship. For anything to move forward, what needs to be established is a relationship of trust and respect between the peoples and the communities. Peace is not just negotiated agreements between politicians. Peace is not just a group of activists sitting together engaging in dialogue or doing a protest every once and awhile. Peace is the process of building trust and respect between the peoples of the land. To be able to see each other with different eyes—new eyes. To be able to really understand who the other is. To appreciate them, their culture, their heritage, the narrative that they bring to the table, even if this narrative is a completely different narrative than the other (as it is in the Holy Land). Trust and respect are the foundations, so Holy Land Trust is about that.

But trust also has another meaning. Trust is also taken from the word trustee. To be a trustee means to take care of a thing until you return it to its rightful owner. If we believe this is holy land, then we have no ownership claim to this land. Only God has claim to this land. We could say this for the Holy Land, and for the world, as well. But let's start with the Holy Land, that little spot. If we are trustees of something, we are to take care of it, we are to maintain it, we are to make it prosper, we are to make it blossom, we are to allow milk and honey to flow in it again—and flow freely, without restrictions, checkpoints, walls, borders, anything. So if we are trustees, we take care of this place and maintain it until its rightful owner claims it back. And that's how we see our work as the organization Holy Land Trust.

Strengthening communities for the future. It's a beautiful statement, but the funny thing about it is that the word *communities* is plural and we made it plural from the beginning. I am Palestinian. All the people who work at Holy Land Trust are Palestinian. We could have easily said "strengthening the community for the future," as a Palestinian organization working for a Palestinian community. Recently it has come to us to understand what we are really meant to do. "Strengthening communities for the future" means for us as people who want to follow the teachings of Jesus that we look at the challenges that face all of the communities of that land—Palestinian, Israeli, Jewish, Muslim, Christian, political parties, whatever they are. What are the challenges they face? And how can we, as the people of this land, provide the answers for them to free themselves and find breakthroughs for the challenges that they each face?

It's not just about the Palestinians. When we talk about peace in the Holy Land it's not just about standing with the Palestinians and asking what we can do to support the Palestinians in their struggle for liberation and ending occupation. It is for all of us, including us as Palestinians, to ask the question: What is missing within the Israeli community that does not allow them to move forward with peace?

When you look at polls that are taken continuously in my land, 70–80 percent of the people want peace, on both sides. What is missing? We've been in this for over sixty-five years now. People are getting sick and tired of hearing about the Palestinian/Israeli conflict over and over again. So what is missing and what is needed to move forward, to once and for all bring peace? Not to come to the tenth annual conference and have the same presentation and same speeches, but instead to say, listen, in the next five years, we're all going to do it, we're all going to work together, and we're going to make peace a reality. To really see what's missing and what's needed and to bring that vision to the land.

So what are the challenges that we face as an organization? And I want to speak now, not just on behalf of Palestinians, but to widen the circle to those who are actively involved in this work, which means many in the evangelical community and the United States. What are the challenges that we need to begin working on?

The biggest challenge, of course, is something called the Occupation—the military occupation of Palestinians by Israel. We as an organization are beginning to take a new look into what this Occupation is about. Historically, if I wanted to give a presentation about this subject I would present a conflict between Palestinians and Israelis, with Israelis being more powerful, occupying the Palestinians, and the Palestinians being the victims, under military occupation. As if it's a struggle between two nations—one fighting for liberation and the other for security. And this struggle is over a piece of land. This is how it's presented. This is what the politicians say, what the media says, and what I said until a couple of years ago.

Now the Occupation is different for me. It's not a "capital O" Occupation, it's a "small o" occupation, dealing with issues that concern our values as Christians. This forces us to get involved in an *occupation* of addressing how people treat each other and how people relate to each other. It is our occupation to address issues of human rights and equality on all sides, the recognition of the other to live and be in this land, no matter their identity. If a Muslim says that no Jews are allowed to live in this land, this is discrimination and needs to be addressed by us. If a Jew says that no Muslim should be on this land, it should be taken at the same level.

So instead of a political conflict that we are engaging in, where we must always try to position ourselves as Christians in terms of who are we with and who are we not with, if we want to do anything good we must ask how we can be a bridge between those two communities. I would challenge us all as Christians to look at the whole thing differently. Not for one or the other, not pro-Palestinian or pro-Israel, but pro-peace, pro-human rights, pro-equality, pro-equal distribution of resources, pro-the right of every religion to worship in their holy sites without restrictions of movement. It's a spiritual struggle between many Israelis and Palestinians who are fully committed to making peace, fully committed to equality, fully committed to justice, over against those who are not, and those who are lost in between. So we need to begin looking at this differently, and this is the challenge. The beauty of this realization is that this is becoming an awakening for many of us who are living in this land.

In October 2012 we organized a big, nonviolent action coming from this new consciousness. Jews, Christians, and Muslims walked together from outside of Bethlehem, from one of the checkpoints, into Bethlehem, into Manger Square. Thousands were there. This was not another one of those political nonviolent protests. We did not even speak. We came with the recognition that we all have rights in this land, and we should treat each other as equals.

Another challenge for us relates to the issue of identity. It was very important for me, as a Palestinian, to begin to understand that when my identity as a Palestinian becomes a hindrance for me to fulfill Jesus' calling for my life, I need to reevaluate. And so I ask you, as well, how do you allow your identity to be either a catalyst for peace work, or a hindrance to the peace work that you should be engaging in? If your identity as an American, as a Christian, or as a representative of an organization becomes a hindrance to following Jesus and a reason for looking negatively at someone else, then I really want to challenge you to consider whether you ought to continue to carry this identity.

For me, it's not about challenging my identity as a Palestinian. But if I use my identity as a Palestinian to blame, to complain, to undermine, to victimize, to attack, to discriminate against, the Israeli and the Jew, then I really have to look into myself and see if this is the identity I want to carry.

Another challenge is our role as activists. We talk a lot, and we listen a lot. And the question is: When will we be able to move from talking to becoming active? To engaging in work, on the ground? This is very important. This is very challenging. Jesus was not just a preacher. He was not just a rabbi who sat in the synagogue all day and spoke. He went out into the community, he engaged the community. He healed people. He stood up for people. He prevented violence from happening when he saw violence was about to happen. He even reached the point of sacrificing his life for us as well. What are the actions that we are ready to engage in that will be challenging? Christians must challenge those who are engaged in violence, from a place of love and compassion, even to the oppressor. For us it is never just about exposing the injustice, and certainly not about engaging in revenge and retaliation. But we must actively challenge injustice and violence.

It's not easy. It has taken me years to move from a place of not being personally involved in a single nonviolent action to a place where if you visited me on a Friday in my office you wouldn't find me, because each Friday I was out on the streets demonstrating and getting beaten up. But I needed to move into this kind of action, certain in my conscience that these actions of non-violence were still in line with what Jesus wanted me to do; if not, I would seek to discern what other actions I needed to do to be aligned with God's will for my life.

In 2012, I was asked by the Israeli military governor of the Bethlehem district to go and meet him for coffee. It's usually an interview about the work we are doing. Captain R. is a man I have known for over ten years. As the captain of the Israeli army brigade, when we would do the nonviolent actions, he would give the orders for his troops to beat us up, to arrest us or to shoot at us. And many times, he would point to me as the leader of the action and say to his soldiers: "Go get him and beat him up." And very interestingly, out of these experiences, we built a wonderful friendship. Amazingly, there was this respect between us, even though he was giving the orders to attack me. And in this interview, he was asking me: "Sami, what are you hiding from me? It's been a couple of years now and I haven't seen you in any demonstration or protest. What's going on?" And I told him: "R., I'm really thinking and praying. How can I express what I want to express in a way that I could show God's love to you?"

Two weeks later, for the first time in thirteen years, I got a permit to go to Jerusalem and Israel. Captain R. issues these permits. I feel that was connected to what I said. He heard something that I think he wants Israelis to hear from me.

A theme of these essays is the issue of love. We are called to love our enemies. No matter what we think, no matter what we feel, no matter how much anger we have in us. No matter how frustrating it is, we are called to love our enemies. My biggest challenge has been not just saying that I love my enemy because Jesus wants me to, but instead to seek to understand just exactly who my enemies are in order to be able to love them. The most transformative experience for me has been going to places like Auschwitz and Birkenau and understanding who my enemy is. I must understand the Holocaust, to understand the suffering, pain, trauma and fear that exists within the Jewish community. The only thing that you can do after that experience is to love them more—to really have compassion for them and understanding of where they came from and where they are now. This is part of what is needed for us, as Christians, to follow the healer of all heal-ers. If Jesus healed pains and traumas, in his name we could heal pains and traumas as well. So healing is an important missing component of the struggle we are in.

So I ask you to continue praying for us, continue supporting us, and continue loving the Palestinian and the Israeli at the same level. They both need our love, our understanding, and our care.

12 Pastors and Peacemaking in a Glocalized World

BOB ROBERTS JR.

THE WORLD IS OPEN to the church like never before—but sadly we are becoming our own worst enemies. The biggest obstacle to us engaging the world with our faith is us. If this book were for clerics of all religions I would write a different essay, but since it is for evangelicals I want to be very specific. We have to deconstruct to build up, because even though we have been contemporizing the church in the West, we still have an old view of faith and how it engages the world.

What you do globally has huge implications for what you do locally. What you do locally has huge implications for what happens globally. One little editorial in the *Washington Post* "On Faith" blog has done more to open global doors for me than anything. Because I was promoting religious freedom for the New York mosque, I've been invited to three "closed" countries to build relationships with clerics, which opens doors for me to talk about faith in their country. I'm not a diplomat or academic but a pastor. That's a very different context, and a massive untapped opportunity.

The journey for me began when our congregation adopted Vietnam and specifically the city of Hanoi as the place we wanted to engage and serve. Doing so would be a radically different paradigm from traditional "missions." People began to use their jobs to serve Hanoi and Vietnam. "Sharing our faith" became more about answering questions to those we were building relationships with than in blanketing an area with gospel tracts. The result is that hundreds of our members have gone, many on a regular basis, to serve the city by using the job skills they learn here to help development there. Another huge impact was with exchange students coming from Hanoi to live with our members in Texas. My biggest challenge came from my strongest Baptist, who asked, "Why are we bringing these atheistic communists here?" It was the greatest thing we could have ever done. It caused us to deal with hard questions not just for them but for us as well. We have had close to one hundred Vietnamese exchange students.

Our church used the exact same approach in Afghanistan, which opened doors for me working with Muslims. I was "outed" as an evangelical early on, which wasn't a bad thing. Everyone knew where everyone stood. It gave us a chance to work together and answer questions as people came to know one another. It ultimately led to me helping other new churches in the United States in adopting that part of the world like we had Vietnam, in the same kind of engagement.

As a result of engaging in this manner, we came to be friends with many of the gatekeepers of the nation. For the most part, we evangelicals have had our "religious" response to peace and foreign affairs, but it isn't enough. Without the Holy Spirit and personal relationships with people from challenging countries, we will be just another group banding together wanting peace. Wanting peace is not enough. We must promote it—and we promote it through relationships. There are five things I would submit to you are very important if as a pastor you are going to work for peace in the world beyond signing a statement.

FROM DISCONNECTED TRIBALISM TO CONNECTED GLOBALISM

I came stumbling into the world. I was the ultimate Western Christian. I could travel the world and never see it. Christians think they are global because they went with their church to another country to work with the church and Christians in another country. It isn't so. I discourage pastors from connecting with the church the first time they travel to a nation they are considering working in. In many instances they can't connect with the church for legal reasons. In other situations, Christianity can be such a fledgling movement in a country that it is very difficult to connect with churches or believers there. I'm also of the opinion that the global church is far healthier than the Western church, and so we must be super careful not to pollute it with the viruses of "Western church disease."

The reality is that everything is in a global public square—there is no privacy anymore. When we band together as Christians to go do "Christian" work in nations and we blog and tweet back home, those blogs and tweets are read by people in those countries.

Those that are twenty-eight and below see the world radically differently than older folk. When we had the Building Bridges and Global Faith Forum at our church, where we had Muslims and Christians coming together in large numbers, we lost two hundred of our older members that had money. We gained over three hundred new members of young families in their twenties—but sadly they're broke! There is an intuitiveness about their world. They've gone to the big "missions" events for young people and their hearts quicken—yet the containers they are put in to engage the world don't fit our current context.

The way we do websites and tweet in the West is frankly offensive to most of the non-Christian world. We have to learn to speak with one conversation, not multiple conversations. How are you going to learn this? Go visit a totally opposite culture. Hanoi or Bethlehem are good places. Instead of witnessing, sit down, be quiet, listen, ask questions, and learn. Be more interested in them than you are in your agenda. Every time you write or tweet, think about what you write or say. How would it be perceived by those you wish to serve? How would that change the way you say it?

If a stuttering Baptist dispensationalist-premillenialist like me can learn, I assure you that you can. Missions as a religious-industrial enterprise will not define Christianity in the twenty-first century, but everyday Jesus-followers will.

From the Gospel of Salvation to the Gospel of the Kingdom

I stumbled into the kingdom. I understood the gospel of salvation—get everybody saved. I had no clue what the gospel of the kingdom was. I came to discover that through a question the Holy Spirit prompted: "When will Jesus be enough?"

The reality is that the world is turned off by religious work and church work. Personal salvation as the ultimate goal is inconsistent with what Jesus taught. Salvation was the starting point, not the ultimate point. I had to see the city and society as the grid on which we operate, instead of focusing on "having" church.

Our response should be to see that the world is open to anyone who wants to serve the city and humanity. The society, not the church, is the grid by which we all operate. We need to attend to *domains*, the infrastructure of how a city or society is built—such as education, government, art, communication, agriculture, health, and economics. If you ask people to go do mission work, they think of Vacation Bible School or an orphan trip—but each person has a job and a skill that is needed in a country. At our church we instead match jobs to jobs, which allows for training, relationship, and development.

The kingdom is where it all starts—the rule and reign of God. Personal salvation is just the entry point. Three words describe the kingdom: transformation, reconciliation, and engagement. The disciple is the center of kingdom action. It isn't the preacher, missionary, or "vocational" religious worker. Our job as "vocational" religious workers is to mobilize the whole body of Christ to do kingdom work, not center them around us.

Next is the city/society. This is the grid we operate on. This is where movement, service, and relationships are built. Finally there is church. It is the gathering of disciples in which equipping and strategic deployment takes place. Church is certainly not just the Sunday event. We have been called to do more than start worship services. The release of the entire body of Christ to enter the domains of city and society must be our goal.

From Compromise to Clarity and Kindness

I came stumbling into the concept of multi-faith engagement. I was getting to know all of these leaders of countries that were different religions than me. I became a novelty item for them—an evangelical pastor who liked them. That would not have been my first preference on how to be known, but that's what happened. They thought it was unique that I was an evangelical pastor and I liked Muslims and Arabs. Often I'd be asked to a part of "interfaith" dialogue. I hated it. Everyone sat around and talked God, but that was it—just talk. Everyone was afraid of offending the other persons present. No one could be honest. It was like we were trying to be politically correct with our theology—and that simply isn't possible without compromising or not being honest. Multi-faith engagement says we have fundamental if not irreconcilable differences between our faiths, but the best of our faiths do teach us that we should get along. So let's be honest, not compromise what we believe, but treat one another with respect.

The reality is we all know we disagree. Religion isn't politically correct. What being "outed" religiously did for me was to cause me to think deeply about what I believed and why I believed it. It also forced me to think hard about how to communicate clearly what I believe. Do I believe in three gods or the Trinity, and if the Trinity, how do I describe it in a way that is core, clear, simple, and understandable? If I can't do that, how can I even believe my own faith?

The word *Christian* doesn't bother me like it does some. I don't want to run from the term. I want to show non-Christians a Christian who loves them and respects them. Otherwise how do I relate authentically to those of other faiths? Truth is never arrogant, haughty, or hateful—people are. Truth is humble and kind and gentle. If we do believe Jesus is the "way, the truth, and the life" (John 14:6) that doesn't produce harshness, arrogance, or mean-spiritedness in how we relate to people of other faiths. If anything, it produces brokenness and compassion.

Clarity is critical for understanding and trust. You don't have to compromise what you believe, just be kind.

From Dialogue among Clerics to Engagement between Congregations

Sadly, in helping people of different faiths get along, it's as if we are stumbling over clerics to get to the masses. The real power is the people.

The reality is that we cannot truly discuss theology without a legitimate relationship unless all we want is academia. Preachers wanting to preach globally are actually a big obstacle. The greatest thing a pastor can do is to mobilize and equip *the church* to engage the world. The greatest power of a pastor is to connect and release his people to engage with people of other faiths. Statistics show you don't have to fear your members converting to another faith. It may actually make them stronger in theirs, as it did for me and my family.

The response we usually have is to first start with the *head* and try to convince someone we don't know to change their faith to ours. Generally this is where the conversation ends. Then we try to become their friend so we can ask more questions and build a *heart* relationship—but this rarely happens. On rare occasions it may lead to using our *hands* in service with the person. I believe the order must be reversed. First, for the common good of our city and the world, we should come together around building one another up in our cities. So start with the hands. Once we are working together and sweating together, we become friends, and it moves to the heart. Once there is a heart relationship, there is trust. Now you're ready to have the conversations, because you know and respect one another as individuals instead of seeing someone as a religious commodity to be had.

Our church has done cooking clubs with people of different faiths, worked in senior centers, rebuilt homes, and countless other projects. These lead to powerful conversations.

From Culture-Driving Majority to Minority-Protecting Majority

I came stumbling from a commitment to religious freedom for Christians to religious freedom for all. I never thought about religious freedom for others—after all, I live in the United States where we have religious freedom. But do Muslims? How do Christians treat Muslims and people of other religions when they want to build places of worship? Freedom of religion in a nation isn't gauged by the freedom experienced by those in the majority religion, but those in the minority religion. Furthermore, what we do here with minority faiths has a direct impact on what people of our faith experience in other parts of the world where they are the minority.

I disagree with Newt Gingrich when he says: "When Saudi Arabia lets us build churches there, then we will build more mosques here." Saudi Arabia isn't my standard. We can and should set the tone, not just around the world, but right here at home.

The reality is that it's up to the majority to reach out to the minority. I was horsing around one day and started tweeting what I love about Muslims. Eboo Patel went crazy over it. I was amazed at how many Muslims were grateful to come to our church for the bridge-building event we did. We hold 2,000 in our building but had over 2,500. The thing I heard again and again was young fathers thanking us for making life better for their children and not looking down on them.

Our response must be to support religious freedom in America for all faiths. What we desperately need in an American president is someone with a "global" perspective. Whether it's the economy, oil, foreign affairs, environment, statecraft, etc., we Americans, sadly, see through a purely "American" or local lens. Our two oceans and two (unrecognized) states above and below us don't do much to help us see and think globally.

Because we have businesses with global outposts and we've traveled to different countries, we think we are global, but we are not. This is my biggest concern for my country. We don't realize how we are contributing to the tension in the world; we always think it is other people's fault, but it's often us. We're hogging the bed because we're so big without realizing others are about to fall off. I am optimistic about the millennial generation, but they won't be in leadership for another fifteen to twenty years. We can't wait that long for a change in perspective. Neither can our world.

13 Loving People Like Jesus Does

DAVID BEASLEY

I SERVED AS GOVERNOR of South Carolina from 1995 to 1999. In 1998 I lost my bid for reelection after trying to take down the Confederate flag and end Indian gambling in South Carolina. I was probably the only person in my administration that was content with losing the election, because I knew that "God causes all things to work together for good" (Rom 8:28, NASB). In fact, Chuck Colson called me after the loss and said, "God has another plan for you."

After the election, some friends and I began talking about the world. We asked ourselves where Jesus was and where he would want us to be. Our attention turned to Islam. We began reaching out to Muslims in other parts of the world, intending to teach them more of the truth about Americans. In the end, Muslims taught me more than I taught them.

One of our projects was to put on free conferences in Yemen, bringing in top speakers to talk about economic development strategies. The conferences were really the secondary purpose; the primary purpose was to get to know one another. We also hoped that they would see Jesus in our lives.

I required the speakers to not only pay their own way, but also to stay a few extra days beyond the conference. I asked this because we needed to do more than just deliver a message of America having all the answers. We needed to spend time with Yemenis and to let them see our hearts. When people spend time together over meals, they begin talking about life and meaningful topics beyond the rhetoric of policy.

At one of these conferences, a Sunni Muslim approached me on the third or fourth day. He was very nervous to be addressing me. His name was Mohammed, and he sat by me and said, "I really don't know much about your faith, but you sound like someone who follows Jesus."

I said, "Well, I'm lousy at it. What about you?"

He answered, "Well, Jesus is in the Koran."

This was one of my early experiences with Muslims, and I did not know much about the Koran. I basically thought that if you touched it, your hand would singe. I was a leader, but similar to many other right-wing, fundamentalist Christians from the South, I had this extraordinary view.

Mohammed told me that Jesus was in the Koran. He said, "In the Koran, Isa (Jesus) is Al-Masih (the Messiah), born of the Virgin Mary."

I said, "You're kidding."

"Isa performs miracles; it's in the Koran."

And I said: "Wow!"

"He's called the Word of God in the Koran. He is the Messiah. He's in heaven now. And he's coming back on Judgment Day."

"All this is in the Koran?"

"Yes."

I said, "Then why are we enemies?"

I suggested that I begin reading the Koran and that he read the Ingeel (Gospels), and he answered that the Ingeel is considered a holy book to Muslims. I was amazed.

It was a journey for me to realize that I needed to die to myself and my Western ways. I love America, and I love the West, but I began to die to things that were superficial and merely cultural. If you die to yourself, you begin to talk like Jesus, think like Jesus, act like Jesus, and love like Jesus. Jesus did not start a Middle Eastern corporation. He just took a handful of guys and a few women, and he began to disciple them. He did not convert them, and he did not train them to convert others. He said, "As you go, make disciples of nations" (Matt 28:19, author's translation).

A friend of mine once said to me, "You need to disciple yourself first if you want to change the world." Disciple yourself first. As you do that, begin to study and analyze how Jesus trained his followers. Jesus said that he had finished the work that the Father had sent him to do, which was to disciple men and women. He spent three years doing that. He could have just come to earth for a day, died on the cross, and then sent the Holy Spirit. So why did he spend three years intimately relating to a small group of men and women? He was teaching them the curriculum, teaching them how to die to themselves, how to start small groups. Yes, every now and then, he gave speeches to small crowds, but every day, every week he was teaching his followers discipleship. Jesus' emphasis was on discipleship, not conversion. Peter is just one example of this. Peter was a long way into his discipleship before he even recognized that Jesus was the Messiah.

Sometimes we think that we have to go out and ram Jesus down people's throats. But Jesus actually teaches that if you want someone to know that you are his disciple, then you should show love. That does not even require words. As St. Francis of Assisi would say: "Preach the gospel at all times, and when necessary use words."

As I saw this in Jesus' life, I began rethinking my approach to making disciples. I began meeting with leaders privately, quietly talking about Jesus, always having someone with me. If I loved the believer that was with me like Jesus loved me, then the leaders we were meeting with would see that we were disciples of Jesus.

When Jesus said that if we lift up his name, he will draw all people to himself, he was not necessarily limiting that to a verbal scenario. Lifting up his name can mean lifting up the love of Jesus in your heart, your mind, and your soul, and being of one mind and one spirit with other believers. In the Garden of Gethsemane, Jesus prayed for believers. He prayed that they would be one, as he and the Father were one. He said that by believers' complete and perfect unity, the world would know that the Father had sent Jesus. So, if I want a leader, a vagabond, a sinner, or an elevator operator to know that Jesus was sent by the Father, and that I am a disciple of Jesus, then all I really need to do is love the person that is with me and be in complete unity with him.

Sometimes it seems that in American society, we Christians do everything we can to accomplish the antithesis of what Jesus taught. Jesus told us to be one, but instead we have Baptists and Methodists and Catholics and Protestants and Orthodox. I do not say this as condemnation, but when the rest of the world sees how divided we are, how does that witness to our unity in Jesus?

Unity in Jesus does not mean political unity. In fact, some of the greatest witnessing to the power of Jesus that I have seen has been between political enemies. There is a small fellowship group of politicians in Washington, DC that meets on Capitol Hill. In this group were two particular senators, a right-wing extremist and a left-wing extremist (as they might call each other). They did not like each other, but they both came to the group. There are no outsiders in that fellowship room. Everyone takes their label off; for that one hour, once a week, they are not Democrat or Republican. No one is chairman of a committee. Everyone is the same. They are all one. They are not male or female, Gentile or Jew, black or white. And these two men, who hated each other, met together like in Acts 2, breaking bread and having fellowship and praying together around Jesus. It took a long time. At first, they sat on opposite sides of the room. Finally one of them said something that caught the other's heart, and a little bit of the wall between them broke down. The process continued until finally, on the floor of the Senate, one of these men said that when he had struggles with family matters and illnesses, the best friend he had in the world was this senator who used to be his enemy. This was a powerful testimony of unity in Jesus.

Two years ago I had a Muslim friend who loved Jesus as much as many of my Christian friends. He knew a Maronite Christian who also loved Jesus. This Muslim and this Christian became friends around Jesus, even though they had their differences. One saw Jesus as a prophet and one saw him as the Messiah. They both now see Jesus as Messiah, even though the one still calls himself a Muslim. I am not worried about that. I just love seeing people coming together and loving each other.

The Muslim met with the Grand Mufti of Lebanon and said, "We need to make friends with these Christians." The Christian met with the Maronite patriarch and encouraged him to meet with the mufti. When they brought these two men together for the first time, their advisors wanted it to be in public, at a press conference. However, my Muslim friend asked them to meet together privately and quietly once a week to pray together, to become friends, and to learn to trust each other first. Two years later, they finally held a press conference together. Everyone there was moved to tears because they could see that these two men truly loved each other. It was powerful.

The stories I am telling give examples of the power of how Jesus works. I would have liked to think that some of my old ways were effective, but I have found that they are not nearly as effective as just loving people unconditionally, whether they are Muslim or Buddhist or Christian or atheist. I have seen atheists come to Jesus by telling them, "I'm not here to convert you, but I would love for you to get to know the man Jesus, who taught a revolution of love."

They say, "I would love to hear more about Jesus if you don't try to convert me."

And I say, "I'm not going to try to convert you. Why don't you just read about him and study about him, and if there is a God, ask him to give you something." Within months, something happens.

At one point, I was meeting with newly-elected members of the Kosovo Parliament. I was meeting with about twenty-five of the one hundred members. Seventeen or eighteen were Muslim; five or six were Orthodox, and a couple were atheists. I said, "I'm here today to talk to you about starting a fellowship program here. We have groups all over the world meeting together, breaking bread, praying together, and having fellowship around Jesus of Nazareth. If you do those four things, you personally will be blessed, and your nation will be blessed."

I expected that most of them thought that I was there to convert them, so I said, "Look, I'm not trying to convert you from this religion to that religion. Jesus never said to be a Christian." That settled them a little bit, and I continued, "You may be an atheist who sees Jesus as just a man, but the teachings of Jesus to love your enemy will revolutionize your nation. Or maybe you are a Muslim, and you see Jesus as a prophet, but the teachings of that prophet to feed the poor and the needy will transform your communities. And maybe you're a Christian. You can gather together around these teachings and this person and not worry about converting one another. Just gather and love each other and address the problems of your nation. You personally will be blessed and your nation will benefit from it."

They began to meet. The atheist was okay with it. The Muslim was okay with it. The evangelical Christian was concerned about it. He approached me afterward and said, "I don't know if I can do that." I suggested that he reread the story of Jesus healing the man blind from birth (John 9). Jesus met with the blind man and gave him sight. The Jewish leaders called him in and said "Who did this to you?"

He said, "A man named Jesus."

They threw him out but called him back later and asked, "Who did this to you?"

Again, he said, "A prophet named Jesus."

They rebuked him, and he said, "Do you want to be his disciple, too?" Then they kicked him out. Jesus encountered him the third time and clearly gave him insight beyond human insight. Then the man worshiped him as a prophet and as a savior, and at that point he became a disciple. I told this hesitant Christian that this story should encourage him to be patient, to lift up the name of Jesus and his teachings, and to trust God for the results.

This is a comprehensive strategy that can change the world. Jesus took a handful of women and men and changed the world. It did not take a big budget. It really just took one-on-one discipleship and loving one another. Practicing this kind of discipleship in pairs is even more powerful. The power of God with one is one thousand. The power of God with two is ten thousand.

The more we die to ourselves, the more he will do through us. He will be lifted up and people will be drawn to the Jesus that is within us. I'm asking each and every one of you to get back into the Gospels. Disciple yourselves first, and have a partner to travel with to show that incredible love.

Once I was with Os Guinness, and I said, "Your books are great, but they're so hard. I can hardly understand them." We laughed, and then I continued, "Os, we really need to get our friends to reread the Gospels again and again. So while you're writing all these great books, please don't let your books become a distraction from the Gospels or a distraction from the Word of God."

Policy only works so much, but the love of God, through Jesus Christ the Messiah, who came for the whole world—that is the answer, and that is the comprehensive peace plan.

14 Where We Have Been— and Where We Go From Here

Jim Wallis

THERE ARE MANY PEACE lovers in this world. Peacemakers are harder to find. Loving peace is just loving the absence of conflict, but peacemaking means learning how to love your enemies, which is very different. Churches have been involved in a number of peacemaking efforts over the last several decades. I would like to give a brief overview of our involvement and of what we learned from these situations.

To begin with, during the conflict in Vietnam, there were a handful of Christian voices, mostly Catholic, which spoke up against the war. A small number of evangelicals also looked at that war and saw that it was wrong. For some of us, that changed our lives and led us into peacemaking.

Christians had a stronger voice during the nuclear arms race. Churches were at the animating core of the Nuclear Weapons Freeze Campaign in the 1980s. We at Sojourners were a part of this campaign that changed American opinions about the nuclear arms race. During that time, Billy Graham visited Auschwitz and had opportunities to preach behind the Iron Curtain. Good preachers fall in love with the people they are preaching to, and when Billy Graham preached behind the Iron Curtain, he realized that our warheads were aimed at his congregations, and their warheads at us. He began to think about what a Christian response to this situation would be. After returning from Poland, he commented that if we continued in our current path (pursuing more and more powerful weapons), Auschwitz would be only a dress rehearsal for the end of the world. His change of opinion about the arms race was also representative of a larger shift going on in America. This shift was one of the reasons the Cold War ended.

We evangelicals had even more influence over the wars in Central America. Witness for Peace was a significant vehicle for this influence. It began while some Christians were visiting Jalapa in the northwest frontier of Nicaragua. While they were there, the mortar shells from the contras (terrorists backed by the United States) stopped. The people of Jalapa asked the American Christians to come back often. In response, Witness for Peace began sending thousands of North Americans to the war zones of Nicaragua. Where they went, the contras stopped shelling. The North Americans returned home changed.

At one point I was in Cleveland, Ohio, meeting with a team that had just returned from Nicaragua. A call came in that Ocotal had just been attacked by the contras. I shared that with the people in Cleveland, and tears came to their eyes. They said, "That's where we just were. Could it be Maria lying dead in the streets? Could it be Jose?" They joined hands and prayed for Nicaraguans, by name, whom they had met. I knew then that the war would soon end. The next day they went to the press, and Cleveland heard the truth about what happened in Ocotal, from the Christians who had just been there. When the contra war funding was defeated in Congress, the State Department blamed the churches, and we were happy to be blamed.

Gustavo Parajon, a now-departed evangelical from Nicaragua, called me one day when I was on a retreat with friends. He called to ask all Christian leaders to stop the invasion of Nicaragua that was being planned by the United States. There were twelve of us on the retreat. I asked him how we could stop the invasion in Nicaragua, and he answered, "I don't know, but we just wanted to call you . . . and pray and . . . would you just please stop it?" So we prayed, and the twelve of us decided that if the United States invaded Nicaragua, we would go into our congressional offices and do civil disobedience until Congress either had a debate or stopped the invasion. We planned to go to our constituencies and ask the same thing of them. Eighty-thousand people signed a pledge of resistance. Half of them were Catholic nuns, which is wonderful. Most members of Congress are intimidated by nuns in their offices, refusing to leave. We didn't have Twitter or email. We had what you call "phone trees." On a phone tree, we could reach 80,000 people in twenty-four hours. We now know one of the main reasons that the United States did not invade Nicaragua was the domestic problem of having to put 80,000 of their own citizens in jail. We helped stop that invasion.

There are numerous other examples. It is clear that South Africa would not have turned out the way it did without the leadership of the churches there and churches in the United States, and their relationship to each other. Other examples are the Sanctuary Movement in El Salvador, the killing of the American church women, and the Jesuit massacre in San Salvador. After the Jesuit massacre, Jesuits here brought pictures of their brothers who were killed. We took them to the White House, and the Jesuits asked me to pray with them there. We did, and we were arrested. These events all had tremendous impact.

Another example was during the first Iraq war. A delegation of religious leaders attempted to talk to Saddam Hussein, to persuade him to withdraw from Kuwait. The group talked to his cabinet, but Saddam refused to meet with them. He appeared to want the war. We came so close, but it did not work.

Before the second Iraq war, the Americans polled were fifty percent for the war and fifty percent against, or sixty percent for and forty percent against, depending on the question asked. That many Americans were against the war in Iraq! The vast majority of evangelicals around the world were opposed to the war in Iraq. So a group of American church leaders met with Tony Blair for over an hour, talking about theology and Jesus and moral arguments. The Cabinet almost decided not to go to war in Iraq. The alternative to war presented in the British Cabinet was the "American Churches Plan." A donor gave us a quarter of a million dollars to put that plan in every newspaper in Great Britain before the debate. The churches were not just opposing the war, they were offering an alternative. Again, we did not win, but we tried, and we came close.

Many of us have also been involved in Palestine and Afghanistan. During the Afghan Surge (2009–2011), leaders from the development community and the churches proposed an alternative called the Development Surge. This plan was based on the input of people who were there, who knew what it would take to rebuild Afghanistan. We offered President Obama a credible plan, but, as a Democrat and the first black president, he felt too trapped by the military to put our plan into action.

"Love your enemies" is the hardest saying of Jesus. It is the hardest issue for Christians. It is the hardest issue for American Christians. It is the hardest issue for evangelical American Christians. The way we define our identity makes it hard for us to love our enemies. I was debating Dinesh D'Souza on American exceptionalism at a very conservative Christian school. They agreed with him politically, but I started by saying: "Let's, from the start, say what we all know to be true. We are Christians first, and Americans second." You could feel the crowd cringe. They knew they could not disagree with that, but it was not really how they felt. Our sociology replaces our theology time and time again.

How many sermons have you heard since September 11, 2001 on this text: "Love your enemies" (Matt 5:44)? What would it mean to wrestle with this text in the face of real threats from real people? Glen Stassen and I used to debate pacifism versus just war from two big pulpits. I was in the pacifist pulpit, of course. Eventually, I came to the conclusion that it was wrong to stand high above the world debating pacifism and just war. I realized that we needed to get down to the ground, down in the streets, and to engage real conflicts. We needed to take loving our enemies down from the pulpit and into the real world. That is what just peacemaking is all about.

Human conflict is inevitable. If you do not believe that, you have bad theology. We have real enemies who mean us harm. When people give me death threats, I take them seriously. There are real threats in the world. Nevertheless, we resolve most of our conflicts without killing anybody. Could we resolve more of them without killing each other?

We need theological answers for our positions on war and peacemaking. I was once debating a Southern Baptist on CNN, and I asked him why he was in favor of the war in Iraq, and his answer was, "We Southern Baptists tend to trust our President." That is not a theological answer. We can have political views, but we need theological answers. I have been writing about this in a new book, *Surprising our Enemies*. The book applies the Bible's teaching about enemies—"But if your enemy is hungry, feed him, and if he is thirsty, give him a drink; for in so doing you will heap burning coals on his head" (Rom 12:20, NASB)—to our present situations. This teaching is about surprising our enemies with love.

Many people in this country now understand that wars of occupation have often failed. Young people and low income people are serving five and six tours of duty. They see atrocities and torture. More veterans commit suicide every day than are casualties of wars. We are putting such stress on these young people, and these wars are not tenable. I expect that we will soon be able to argue that war is obsolete as a way to resolve human conflict.

If war is indeed becoming obsolete and unsustainable, how should we deal with real threats? I see policing as a viable alternative. John Yoder, a pacifist, says that the difference between policing and war is limits, rules, frameworks, and restraints. International peacemaking would need to make use of force. Use of force is part of Romans 13, but there are rules. Torture is not one of them. Killing innocent civilians is not one of them. We need to cease using special forces with no restrictions or rules and instead implement a new form of international policing and peacemaking.

There are limits to governmental conflict resolution, but people of faith can bring our creativity to bear for the sake of peace. We can show courage, take risks, put ourselves in difficult and dangerous situations. As the global body of Christ, we can make friends and build relationships that lead to peace.

In 2010 Daisy Khan and Feisal Abdul Rauf were in the middle of the conflict over their plans to build a mosque near Ground Zero. A pastor from Florida had threatened to come to New York and to burn Qur'ans on September 11 unless they cancelled the mosque project. Daisy called me, worried about Feisal. I said, "Have Feisal leave town; we'll figure something out." "Oh thank you, thank you," she said. I found myself in a bind; it was Friday, September 10th, and I had commitments I could not get out of. How was I going to help? Just then I got a call from Geoff Tunnicliffe, saying, "Jim, I just wanted to give you a call because I want to help your friend, the imam (Feisal)." Talk about a call from the right person at the right time! I called Daisy and said, "Someone is going to call you. Trust him like you trust me." She and I had built trust in each other, and that trust was able to expand. That is how relationships work toward peacemaking.

Stories began to appear on CNN, MSNBC, and Fox, and the message was, "My friends aren't terrorists, and you shouldn't burn Qur'ans." It was a positive, exciting message. I wanted CNN to continue telling positive stories of people making peace. Finally, CNN agreed to tell the story of Heartsong Church, outside of Memphis, Tennessee, in a suburb called Cordova.

Steve Stone, an evangelical pastor, heard that an Islamic cultural center was coming to his neighborhood, so he put up a big sign that said, "Heartsong Church Welcomes Islamic Cultural Center." The local Muslims were astonished. They came the next day and tentatively knocked on the door. They said, "We were hoping to be ignored, but you welcomed us. Why?"

"Because," Steve said, "Jesus tells us to love our neighbors and even our enemies. We don't know much about Islam, but we'd like to learn."

Before long, the barbeques had halal meat, kids were playing together, Muslims and Christians were tutoring and working with the homeless together. When Ramadan came, the Islamic Cultural Center was not finished, so the Muslims asked if they could use the church basement for their Ramadan gatherings. Steve said: "No, you can meet in the sanctuary." This pastor and imam trust and love each other, while still each holding to their own beliefs.

After the story had aired on CNN, I called Steve, and he told me that he had received a phone call from a group of men in Pakistan.

"Is this the pastor?" they asked.

"Yes."

"We watched that segment on CNN. We were silent for a long time, and then one of us said, 'I think God may be speaking to us through this man.' Another one said, 'How can we kill these people?'"

After seeing the piece on CNN, one of the men had gone to a little church near their mosque, and with his Muslim hands, he had washed and cleaned the inside and outside of that church. Then the men congregated in a room at 1:30 in the morning to call this pastor that they had seen on television. They said to him, "We want you to tell your congregation, Pastor, that we don't hate them. We love them, and because of what you've done, we're going to look after that little church for the rest of our lives."

So what works in the midst of international conflict and violence? Drones? Or proactive love? What we believe is not just a theory or an academic notion; it is a practical strategy for making peace in the world.

In August 2012, a mosque in Joplin, Missouri was burned down. Our Sojourners team decided to put up a billboard three miles away from the mosque. The billboard said, "Love your Muslim Neighbors." That is all it said, but it drew a lot of publicity. Putting the right message in the right place at the right time can make all the difference.

Walter Jones is a conservative congressman from North Carolina. He is on the armed services committee, and he voted for the war in Iraq. He did not really trust the intelligence, but he knew that if he voted against the war, with 50,000 retired military in his district, he would not be reelected. So he voted for the war. As the war progressed, he started going to the funerals of soldiers who were killed. He saw mothers with children who would not have their fathers anymore. He met wounded soldiers. He now calls his vote for the war in Iraq a sin. He has written a letter to every family member of every fallen man or woman. He has written over 10,000 letters as penance for his vote. Now he leads the effort among Republicans to stop the war in Afghanistan. He calls us to humility in our views about these issues.

Our faithfulness leads to effectiveness. We start by just being faithful, but if we are faithful to what Jesus says, we can and will be very effective. I teach at Georgetown on Tuesdays, and I walked in the other day and saw the sign for this summit. It said, "Evangelicals for Peace." I thought, "This is cool." But do you know what a difference evangelicals could make for peace in the world? We might actually love Jesus enough to do what he says when he tells us that we should love our enemies. We will work for peace because of Jesus' promise—that peacemakers would be called children of God.

15 Evangelicals for Peace

RICK LOVE

WHAT WOULD IT LOOK like if we mobilized evangelicals to work towards a biblical, comprehensive, and proactive approach to peace?

Certainly this would mean that we would continue to focus on foreign policy. The challenge is enormous and the potential exciting. In fact, this may be the key area where we need to partner as organizations for the greatest influence. But for the long-term impact of evangelicals for peace, we also need to help the church see how God's peace purposes impact all of life.

For example, one of the issues that we haven't dealt with in this collection of essays is violence in the streets. I live in Colorado, where we have had two mass murders, most recently in Aurora. Twelve people were killed and fifty-eight injured. A commitment to a comprehensive peace means we cannot just focus on preventing war. We need to consider ways to prevent and decrease the multiple forms of violence in our cities.

Another big challenge relates to violence done against women. In 2011 three women were awarded the Nobel Peace Prize: the President of Liberia, Ellen Johnson Sirleaf; Liberian activist Leymah Gbowee; and Yemeni activist Tawakkol Karman. The three Laureates, all women and all mothers, valiantly engage in nonviolent struggle for women's rights. How can we equip the church to engage more effectively in this arena? How can we amplify the voice of women peacemakers?

An additional challenge: how can we mobilize more evangelicals to do peacemaking? This is a huge problem due to a narrow understanding of the gospel and the great commission on the part of many. Let me overstate things to make my point: peacemaking is for liberals, evangelicals evangelize!

I think the statement from the World Evangelical Alliance on "Peace and Reconciliation" says it well:

> God's mission is the reconciliation of all things through Christ, and He invites us to participate with Him in the pursuit of right relationships. We honor the faithful examples of peacebuilding and reconciliation in our history. We confess and repent of our failure, whether through our action or inaction, to bear witness to the Gospel by faithfully living out the peaceable ways of Jesus Christ. In particular, we acknowledge that in our zeal for evangelism, we have often overlooked the biblical mandate to pursue peace. We commit ourselves anew to this mandate within our homes, churches, communities, and among the nations.[1]

I was a missionary prior to becoming a peacemaker. So people often ask me now, "What does your organization do?" My response: we are pioneering what it means to be evangelical peacemakers. We are truly peacemakers and we are truly evangelical. We share the gospel of peace and we pursue the peace of God. But we don't do peacemaking as an evangelistic strategy. It is not a means to an end. Peacemaking has great value in and of itself.

I was talking about peacemaking at a meeting when a woman exclaimed, "But if people don't come to Christ, everything else is worthless!"

What a strong statement. Really? Worthless? Everything else is totally worthless? What then is the relationship between peacemaking and sharing the good news? How do followers of Jesus live out the ministry of reconciliation?

Ideally peacemaking and sharing the good news should be integrated. In practice, however, peacemaking and sharing the good news don't always go together. There are times when someone is reconciled to God but fails to reconcile with his or her neighbor. That's why my organization puts on seminars on interpersonal peacemaking! There are far too many "professing" followers of Christ who fail to make peace with their neighbors, much less their enemies.

There are other instances when making peace between neighbors enables us to effectively bear witness to Jesus. People are drawn to the goodness of the gospel when they see our lights shine in this way. They want to know about the good news of God's reconciling love in Christ. And they decide to follow Jesus.

1. World Evangelical Alliance, "Peace and Reconcilation."

Sometimes, however, people rejoice in the peace made between them and their neighbors but do not want to follow the Prince of Peace. In this case, the good deed of peacemaking still finds favor with God. For Jesus says, "Let your light shine before others that they may see your good deeds, and glorify your Father in heaven" (Matt 5:16, TNIV). The good deed of peacemaking glorifies God and that is not worthless!

So what would a biblical, comprehensive, proactive peace witness look like in practice? I would suggest that it involves six spheres: personal, interpersonal, social, urban, national, and international. Each of these six spheres of peacemaking is biblical, each builds on and encompasses the previous sphere, and each is more complex than the former. The following typology describes my understanding of the scope of peacemaking for evangelicals.

PERSONAL PEACE

We experience peace with God when we enter into relationship with him through Christ. The gospel is explicitly described as the gospel of peace five times in the New Testament. Thus, sharing the gospel of peace is one way we help people experience personal peace. Personal peace also comes through the practice of spiritual disciplines, especially as we pray, walk by faith, and live in peace with others.

INTERPERSONAL PEACE

We experience interpersonal peace as we proactively pursue peace with others by taking responsibility for our wrongdoing, accepting reproof, asking for forgiveness, reproving those who have wronged us, and forgiving them.

SOCIAL PEACE

Group conflict often arises out of cultural, racial, or religious differences, which then leads to prejudice, fear, hatred, ignorance, and misunderstanding. Some of the most prominent group conflicts include gender conflict, class conflict, religious conflict, racial conflict, and conflicts over sexual orientation. The commands to pursue peace and love one's enemy provide the foundation for social peacemaking.

URBAN PEACE

Urbanization is one of the defining traits of the modern world. Over half the world now lives in cities. Jeremiah describes a relevant paradigm for urban ministry: "Seek the welfare [*shalom*] of the city where I have sent you into exile, and pray to the LORD on its behalf; for in its welfare you will have welfare" (Jer 29:7, NASB).

Urban peace—seeking the *shalom* of the city—is broader and more complex than interpersonal or social peace. It includes peace with God, social harmony, health, economic prosperity, and human flourishing. God called these Jewish exiles to seek the common good of the cities where they lived. In New Testament terms, God was calling them to be salt and light, to glorify God through their loving deeds of service to those outside of the faith (Matt 5:13–16). Urban peace involves working with the government and all types of organizations for the common good of the city. It reflects a comprehensive and multi-dimensional peacemaking approach to the city.

NATIONAL PEACE

Most of today's wars are civil wars, not international wars. Countries like Sudan, Somalia, Nigeria, and Sri Lanka immediately come to mind. These national conflicts usually have a variety of triggers. Weak, corrupt, or oppressive government, ethnic diversity, religious diversity, human rights violations, and poverty are the most common. Even though many of these clashes begin as national conflicts, they often escalate and spill over into surrounding nations, endangering their security and resulting in complex humanitarian emergencies. So a national peace problem often becomes an international peace problem.

But even in nations where no literal wars are going on, significant conflict takes place and peacemaking becomes necessary.

Making peace at the national level encompasses urban peacemaking practices along with robust political engagement. The church needs to find formal and informal ways to influence the state.

INTERNATIONAL PEACE

Peacemaking at this level usually involves complex interaction between international, regional, and local actors to mitigate, manage, or resolve conflict. This is often referred to as multi-track diplomacy. Track one focuses on top leaders, usually government to government interaction. The United Nations and other international and regional organizations are also involved at this level. Track two focuses on middle-level leaders or non-state actors (International NGOs, churches, schools, and private businesses). Track three refers to grassroots leaders (indigenous peacemakers and local actors). Formal mediation tends to be the most common method of peacemaking, especially at a track-one level. The Common Word dialogue at Yale University would be an example of track-two international peacemaking.

Few individuals are called to embrace or practice peace in such a comprehensive manner. Thus, it is more accurate to say that the six spheres of peacemaking describe the role of the church universal. God's people from around the globe engage in all six of these spheres depending on their calling. Nevertheless, God calls individuals to grow in their practice of peace—which means that he will often lead us into other spheres.

Sisters and brothers in Christ, what is the future of Evangelicals for Peace? Is this just a book or will we ignite a movement? Will we walk together? Will we work together? Will we pursue peace in these six spheres together? This sounds like a mandate for evangelicals for peace.

16 Evangelical Peacemakers

A Critical Analysis

David P. Gushee

My purpose in this concluding chapter is neither to bury nor to praise the authors of this collection, but instead to push into serious critical analysis of everything we find here. Evangelical peace and war thinking, as well as evangelical on-the-ground peacemaking efforts, matter quite a bit. They matter for reasons that have been enumerated or at least suggested along the way, and which I would summarize as follows:

- The world is actually quite religious today, and so evangelical activity in relation to issues of justice and peace is significant as one species of such religiosity-in-action;

- Evangelicalism is arguably the most vibrant sector of global Christianity, and evangelicals constitute a significant slice of the world's population;

- As a form of religion, evangelicalism's passion and zeal tends to make its religiosity serve as a kind of *accelerant*, for good or ill; thus it is important for evangelical leaders to direct this religion's energies in the most constructive ways possible;

- Evangelical passion and devotion to God (and suspicion/rejection of secularism) sometimes evokes appreciative recognition on the part of seriously passionate and devoted believers in other traditions, notably Islam (the same sense of recognition often goes the other way as well); this gives evangelicals the potential to be effective dialogue partners with the leaders, clerics, and people of nations characterized by profound religious devotion;

- Evangelicals are especially influential in the United States, which remains at the time of this writing the most powerful and most militarily active nation in the world;

- Evangelicals are a growing proportion of the population in many parts of the world in which conflict and war are endemic and sometimes deeply connected to sectarian differences;

- Evangelicalism as a movement does not have and never has had a single position on the ethical issue of war;

- Evangelicals are already engaged in significant individual, congregational, NGO, and state-level diplomacy, activism, and service in relation to war and peacemaking, so it makes sense to try to make those efforts effective rather than just numerous.

While I do not know the precise religious commitments of each author in this collection, it is fair to describe the authors as a whole as representing "evangelical peacemakers"—thus the title of the book. The collection exudes evangelical religiosity in its biblicism, Christ-centeredness, moral seriousness, missionary spirit, and desire to love neighbors near and far in obedience to Christ's command. Each author in one way or another is attempting to represent, advance, or describe evangelical peacemaking. This is true in both major sections of the book: the first four essays, which primarily engage the theology and ethics of peace and war, and the remainder of the essays, which primarily describe evangelical peacemaking efforts on the ground. Let me critically engage each of these in turn.

EVANGELICAL APPROACHES TO WAR, PEACE, AND PEACEMAKING

One can define evangelicalism in historical, theological, institutional, or even ethological terms. Evangelicalism can be seen as classic Protestantism or as a later Protestant renewal movement. Its origins can be traced to the Reformation, or to recurrent renewal movements in European and American Christianity, or to the post-1920s fundamentalist-modernist split in Anglo-American Protestantism, or to the post-World War II birth of neo-evangelicalism out of fundamentalism. Evangelicalism can be defined by its theological commitments, its self-labeling institutions and practitioners, or a particular spirit and ethos that insiders expect and create again and again. But however evangelicalism is defined, it is fair to say that this particular version of global Protestant Christianity has not developed its own independent theology or ethic related to violence and war. Instead, evangelical Christianity has inherited broader Christian theological-ethical tradition/s that are the common heritage of the church universal.

These traditions are described in many textbooks merely in terms of two primary options: *pacifism* and *just war*. We will take Lisa Sharon Harper (ch. 2) as representing a pacifist voice (or tendency) in this collection, while Eric Patterson (ch. 3) articulates a robust defense of just war theory, parts of which I also echo at the end of my chapter (ch. 1). Persistent efforts led by Glen Stassen (ch. 4), sampled here, have added *just peacemaking* to the mix. An honest Christian historical memory would require us to include the *crusade ethic*—holy war in the name of God—which has mobilized the Christian imagination in recurring waves through much of our history, including in some American Christian sectors after 9/11. (That posture is implicitly rejected in this volume, and I explicitly reject it here.) Stassen points out that most Americans simply default to support whatever war an American President says we need to make at a given time. Because most Americans claim also to be Christians, this means that the de facto American Christian approach to war is simply *if my President says we need a war or are at war I will support the President*, which is obviously not representative of any classic Christian theoretical option but shows what really goes on, just the same. If the first four chapters of this collection can help more evangelical Christians actually *think with the Christian tradition* on this matter of the ethics of war, rather than just rally 'round the flag, that itself will have made these four chapters worth the effort.

Jesus against Violence: The Pacifist Commitment

Lisa Sharon Harper's essay begins with the horrible events of 9/11, and it is best to view her chapter as reflecting events in the U.S. during the Bush-Cheney years more than as a comprehensive theoretical explication of a Christian theology of war. However, there is enough biblical and theological content in the essay to reflect on the rudiments of a contemporary evangelical pacifist perspective.

Harper begins with Jesus. She starts with epigraphic quotes from Jesus related to love of enemies and putting away the sword. She then situates Jesus in his context as a subject of terroristic imperial Rome in occupied first-century Palestine. She rightly places him as a Jew living among people mainly desperate to overthrow the Roman overlord-terrorists in their midst. But this Jesus, in this context, refused the Zealot option. Instead he taught, as "literal ethical guidance," turning the other cheek, enemy-love, and peacemaking. And then he exemplified what he taught when arrested by Rome and its collaborators. He allowed himself to be executed cruelly on a Roman cross. He rejected violence at every point in his journey.

Why did Jesus take this path? Harper writes:

> [I]n the faces of the chief priests, and their slaves, and the Roman soldiers, and Caesar himself, Jesus saw the image of God . . . How could Jesus strike down the image of God? He came to redeem and restore the image of God on earth, to set the slaves, and the soldiers, and the priests free from the violent reign of men. He came that Caesar himself might be brought back to life by the dominion of God . . . [S]cripture paints a picture of God's kind of dominion. It is characterized by disciplined power, servant leadership, truth-telling, just dealing, reconciliation and reparation, and above all else love. I believe Jesus did not fight because Jesus believed in redemption.

For Harper, there appear to be two paths: the path of violent conquest, and the path of redemptive love. God, who is sovereign over this world, has through Jesus Christ demonstrated a divine choice to rule through redemptive love rather than violent conquest. We are called to follow the trail that Christ blazed, and to embrace reconciliation, love, and peacemaking. This is Christ's way, and it is the only way to redemption.

But that is not the path that we chose after 9/11, says Harper. We chose conquest. We embraced a war paradigm. That war paradigm embraced all of the pernicious dualisms that usually occur during times of war, such as (we are) good versus (they are) evil, us versus them, and friends versus enemies. The war paradigm involves the embrace of violence and the rejection of legal constraints. After 9/11 it got us not only war but also torture, civil liberties violations, and the militarization of U.S. society. We rejected the path of law and peacemaking and chose "the licentiousness of war." We can and must do better, Harper concludes.

The fundamental strength of the historic Christian pacifist perspective is its rooting in the life, teachings, and example of Jesus Christ. Christian pacifism is Jesus-centered. It takes his specific teachings seriously. It pays attention to his nonresistance to the cruel death inflicted on him at the cross. Harper adds a contextualizing attention to the particularly terrorizing environment of Roman imperial rule, thus drawing a connection to our own fearful response to the terror inflicted on the U.S. on 9/11. And still, even in his terrorizing context, Jesus rejected the path of the sword, a path readily available to him and around him. *The Achilles heel of any Christian perspective toward war that embraces the moral legitimacy of violence is that it is quite hard to square with the life, teaching, and example of Jesus Christ.*

Harper could have gone on to describe the nonviolent witness of the early Christians. This witness is described and advocated in the rest of the New Testament and in postbiblical teaching documents. It is attested to by outside non-Christian observers, usually with scorn. There is no evidence of any Christian participating in the Roman military until the late second century, and no evidence of widespread participation until after the conversion of Constantine in the early fourth century. These historical claims can be quibbled with, and often are, but in my view they hold up under rather strict scrutiny.[1]

Thus on one side of the balance sheet, in favor of pacifism or total Christian rejection of violence, one has both the life and witness of Jesus and the practice of the earliest Christians. For some Christians in all ages and in our age, that evidence is sufficient to settle the matter.

There are powerful arguments for alternative perspectives, however.

One counter-argument grants that Jesus taught and lived peace, as Harper rightly says, but then refuses to grant the applicability of his "private" witness to the "public" life of nations, states, or other collective political entities. The dictates of Christian morality don't really apply to the bloody affairs of nations. Consider this statement from political theorist Robert D. Kaplan:

> Ensuring a nation's survival sometimes leaves tragically little room for private morality. Discovering the inapplicability of Judeo-Christian morality in certain circumstances involving affairs of state can be searing. The rare individuals who have recognized the necessity of violating such morality, acted accordingly, and taken responsibility for their actions are among the most necessary

---

1. Gushee, *Sacredness of Human Life*, ch. 4.

leaders for their countries, even as they have caused great unease among . . . well-meaning intellectuals who . . . make choices in the abstract and treat morality as an inflexible absolute.[2]

One response to Kaplan's "realist" perspective would be to say that while statesmen and stateswomen may look at the world this way, such a posture is ruled out for those who claim to be followers of Christ. Christians—collectively in the church and also as individuals in society—can never exclude the relevance of the witness of Jesus Christ. Quite the contrary: if Jesus Christ is *our Lord*, we Christians are obligated to obey his teachings and imitate his life. And if Jesus Christ is *Lord of all*, we Christians are obligated to seek the implementation of his will in every corner of the world, even now. This would apply to governmental leaders as well, if they are Christians. But Kaplan's comments do point out the sometimes agonizing difficulty of aligning the teachings of Christ with the exigencies of protecting a nation's survival.

Harper falls into a common error on the pacifist side in her essay by failing to consider any kind of distinction between the church and the state. By taking this approach she certainly avoids "ethical dualism," which she decries. But never in her essay does she clarify that "we" the church might have different responsibilities than "we" the state, or those who serve the state as policymakers. In her essay she says that "we" chose the path of conquest and violence and instead suggests that "we" should have chosen the path of redemptive love. (I left "we" language intentionally vague a few paragraphs back in my exposition of Harper to illustrate the issue.) But what if "we" the leaders of the United States government were obligated to pursue the self-defense of the people of the United States, a responsibility that does not fall to "we" the church or its leaders? What if there is a distinction between a nation's leaders performing their obligation to provide for legitimate self-defense and that same nation rounding the bend to "violent conquest" or "revenge," to use Harper's terms? What if it is not part of the vocation of governmental leaders to pursue redemptive love, but instead to defend the security of their citizens as they get on airplanes and ride elevators in tall office buildings? These questions must be considered carefully.

This is not to say that the political leaders of the United States after 9/11 performed admirably in all respects. They did face choices, and Harper and I are not alone in concluding that they sometimes chose very badly. They could indeed have chosen a "legal paradigm" rather than a

2. Kaplan, "The Statesman," 73.

"war paradigm" for assessing and responding to 9/11, as Harper suggests. (Though a legal paradigm is still not a participation in redemptive love, and it does not rule out violence in legitimate self-defense.) Our nation's leaders could have chosen to adhere to the rule of law in how they treated and tried detainees, rather than succumbing to the false belief that torture and indefinite detention without trial were somehow now required to secure the nation, contrary to 225 years of American tradition, law, and practice. Much as I suggested in my own essay (though with regard to a longer timeframe), the abuses and excesses of Bush-Cheney "War on Terror" policies appear to have obscured from Harper's view the more primal and perennial questions about whether followers of Jesus Christ can ever support state violence. One can, as a Christian, take Jesus seriously by seeking peace, supporting the rule of law, opposing excess American militarization, and rejecting torture, and yet still believe in the possibility of a legitimate or even mandatory use of force to defend the lives of innocent people at home or abroad. At least, many Christians have believed precisely this through the ages, and many do today, including our collection's primary expositor of just war theory, Eric Patterson.

Justified Violence as Love of Neighbor: The Just War Tradition

Patterson offers a defense of just war theory based on well-attested Christian tradition, on the vocation of government officials to secure justice, order, and peace, and on the biblical principle of neighbor-love. He contrasts just war adherents with "holy warriors" on the one hand and "radical (or naive) pacifists" on the other. He argues strongly for evangelicals to begin their reflection on war with the "normal and normative" just war position that dominated the church for "1800 years" (better to say 1650, but that's quibbling.) In an email to me, Patterson asked me to "make it clear that at least one voice in this book takes a quite different stand from the left-of-center position, a stand rooted in the historic just war tradition and much more comfortable with the currents of U.S. responsibility and power than most of the other chapters." I honor that request here.

The antiquity of the just war tradition is unquestionable. Its roots precede Christianity, and it began its long, slow journey of development within the Christian faith with the fourth-century leaders Ambrose and Augustine. It is indeed the majority voice in church history from that time forward until today.

That antiquity, of course, does not extend into the pages of the New Testament, and no one claims that Jesus himself took a "just war" position—though C. S. Lewis imagines him doing so in a quote Patterson offers in his chapter. If we are arguing purely about antiquity, the early, pre-Ambrose/Augustine church gets the nod, which is one reason why those in favor of just war approaches devote considerable attention to figuring out other reasons besides Christ-imitating rejection of violence to explain why the early church opposed Christian military service. The explanation offered by Charles and Demy and cited by Patterson, that it had to do with the religious accoutrements of military service in the pagan Roman imperial forces, is a partial truth. Clearly the earliest Christians faced a chronic struggle related to participating in a Greco-Roman culture drenched in paganism, and often in emperor-worship; it was the same struggle faced by the Jewish community, but with less toleration from Rome. This explanation does not account, however, for the clear, wide-ranging, and comprehensive anti-violence teachings of the Church Fathers well into the fourth century.[3]

Why not say instead that the growth in the number of Christians in the Roman Empire, then the conversion of Constantine under the Christian banner, then the toleration of Christianity, and finally the establishment of Christianity as the religion of the Empire, irrevocably altered the posture not just of the Roman Empire to the church but also of the church toward the Roman state and its successors? A state that was no longer enemy but protector of Christians, and not just protector of Christians but defender of orthodox Christianity, and finally defender of orthodox Christianity against the barbarian hordes coming from the north and west, just *looked different* to the fourth- and fifth-century church (and thereafter) than the emperor-worshipping and Christian-harassing regime of earlier times.

And so with Ambrose and Augustine the church began its long, fateful journey of attempting both to bless and to restrain the hand of the state in relation to its violent efforts to provide security and order to its people. The church would not challenge the responsibility of sovereign authorities to deter aggression and to punish it. Church leaders would classify that responsibility as God-given, with scriptural attestation, such as Romans 13 and 1 Peter 2, which Patterson cites. The church's role now would be to advise state leaders on the responsible use of force. It would ask kings and empresses whether military actions under consideration met all relevant

3. Gushee, *Sacredness of Human Life*, ch. 4.

criteria. Once initiated, the church would continue to monitor military activity to be sure that moral restraints were maintained. And perhaps the church's main role would be in its moral formation efforts in a Christian civilization in which both kings and peasants were baptized and trained in the church's moral traditions.

Just war tradition was a product of Christendom. It was a combination of classic Greco-Roman reasoning together with biblical resources, rooted in the Athens and Jerusalem synthesis that characterized Christendom at its apotheosis, and in service of self-consciously Christian civilizations. Some of the church's most elegant thinkers provided some of its most elegant expositions, including thinkers such as those named by Patterson in his well-informed essay. Augustine, Aquinas, Luther, Calvin, Bonhoeffer, Lewis, Niebuhr, Ramsey . . . they all took their shots at describing and advancing the theological ethics of the just war in Christendom.

The twentieth century may have represented the climax of the just war tradition, in this sense: the obvious evil of the ungodly fascist and communist regimes that ravaged our world from 1917 until the fall of the Soviet Union emerged at precisely the time in which secularism was undercutting at their roots what had once been Christian civilizations. But it was still quite possible for a Bonhoeffer in Germany, a Lewis in England, or a Niebuhr or Ramsey in the United States, to consider their side's wars against Nazism and Communism to be just wars against evil and in defense of (something like) Christian nations and Christian civilization.

Those kinds of mid-century Black Knight adversaries offer the best-case scenario for just war thinking. Against genocidal tyrants like Hitler and Stalin it becomes very difficult to defend non-resistance or even nonviolent resistance. It also becomes difficult to conflate the relative moral weaknesses and sins of countries like Great Britain and the United States with the near-absolute evils of a Nazi Germany or Soviet Union, though offering moral equivalencies is a perennial temptation on the pacifist side. Countries that have gone over to the darkness in such radical ways must be resisted by those that have not. Our very effort to honor the restraints of just war theory against societies guilty of so much mass murder becomes one demarcation line between our side and theirs.

Patterson's essay reflects very well-worn grooves in the road of Christian thought, to wit: we live in a fallen world, not the eschatological era in which lions lie down peaceably with lambs. In such a fallen world security is a constant challenge, and when people are able to live in peace and security it is a profound communal and governmental achievement. Such orderly, secure peace does not happen on its own but requires guardians, notably armed forces directed by vigilant and responsible political leaders, who will never and can never be pacifists. Just war theory on Patterson's view is the best tradition available in Christianity that can account for both the world that we find ourselves actually living in and the moral aspirations (and expectations) articulated in the Bible. It recognizes the need to restrain evil by threatening and sometimes using force while placing restraints on the restrainers. It's not just anything goes for national security, not even at the motivational level. Just war theory as presented by Patterson and the best voices of that tradition carries a certain kind of moral stringency that appeals to the Christian conscience, ennobling the theoreticians who write about it and the policymakers who seek to live according to its terms.

But I suggested earlier that just war theory may have climaxed with World War II. What I mean is that the defeat of Nazism did not leave us much of Christendom, which more or less disintegrated, and not just because of Auschwitz. The Allied powers themselves committed massive violations of *jus in bellum* criteria, for example, in the bombing of civilian population centers. The postwar world saw the rapid advance of a disillusioned and/or consumerist secularism. Few thoughtful people would today declare Western Europe or the United States "Christian civilizations." The twilight Cold War struggle with the Soviet Union involved an awful lot of vicious play on both sides. Islamist terror attacks briefly helped at least some American Christians to recover their inner crusader, but the nastiness of Abu Ghraib and the 2002–2003 Torture Memos made it difficult to celebrate U.S./American Christian virtue very readily. And few could argue that U.S. policymakers in recent decades have been consulting their *City of God* or *Summa* when crafting U.S. military policies.

I am suggesting that just war theory was a product of Christendom, the era of "Christian civilization" that has now passed. It was never as pristine in reality as it appeared on parchment. An awful lot of blood was spilled during that Christendom era by men whose leaders *on all sides* were certain that theirs was a just cause. All the just war theory in all of Christendom didn't prevent the abuses of the Crusades or later Christian moral debacles, up to and including all those Christian countries slaughtering their way through World War I, not to mention Dresden and Hiroshima. And those who have implicitly or explicitly classified the United States as the latest virtuous Christian civilization locked in conflict with today's latest Black

Knights are probably not paying a lot of attention to what has been going on in the shadows of our foreign and military policy since the Cold War.

Ultimately, the greatest internal Christian challenge to just war thinking rests with the haunting witness of Jesus himself. I say this as one who finds just war theory in many ways quite compelling. Recall that I closed my own essay with a vignette in which I quite easily imagined how it might be my responsibility someday to use violence to protect innocent people. But still: Jesus comes preaching the dawning of God's kingdom (cf. Matt 4:17), and just war theory gives little evidence that any kind of new kingdom is on its way. It's the same old broken world, only with violence somewhat restrained rather than unmitigated. That's it. Jesus does not teach or personally take up the way of violence, but just war theory calls Jesus into service of violence through extrapolative application of his pivotal teaching that we are to love our neighbors (cf. Matt 22:36–40). We are to love our enemy-neighbors when we are killing them (if necessary) to prevent them from doing evil. We are to love our victim-neighbors when we are protecting them by killing their enemies. It all makes great sense, except no one can dare to say that Jesus himself actually loved neighbors in these ways. The fact that Jesus praised a Roman centurion for his faith or that John the Baptist didn't disarm the soldiers he encountered is utterly peripheral to this fundamental biblical problem. It will never go away as long as people take seriously both the actual life, ministry, and teachings of Jesus Christ, and the continuing presence among us of evildoers who steal, kill, and destroy innocent human lives.

And then there is this. Those we elect and train to protect innocent lives all too often slip loose of the moral and legal restraints we place upon them. They become the next round of tyrants and murderers, who must therefore be restrained by the next round of political and military officials/restrainers, who all too easily can become the next round of tyrants and murderers, who must be restrained by the next round of vigilant and responsible government and military officials, who . . . and the beat goes on. Meanwhile, looking upon the whole sorry lot of us is Jesus Christ, the crucified God. Surely he has something to teach us that goes beyond even the best insights that have been distilled into 1600 years of just war theory.

Faithful and Effective: Just Peacemaking Practices

Eric Patterson is a distinguished contemporary exponent of the 1600-year-old just war theory. Glen Stassen has the distinction of being the *creator* of just peacemaking theory. Again and again he has returned to its themes in his writings over the past twenty years. Meanwhile he has been building first an ecumenical and now an interfaith community of scholars collaboratively seeking to refine and advance its principles and practices. But just peacemaking is an infant compared to the aged just war theory. This is one reason why there are still, quite unfortunately, numerous expositors of "the Christian ethics of war" who do not mention just peacemaking even in their book-length works. By now, that is just bad scholarship.

Glen Stassen's rendering of just peacemaking in this volume is a much-abbreviated version of his longer essays and books on the theme. I will try to offer a restatement based in part on my reading of the broader body of his works on the subject.

Just peacemaking begins with realism about the constant emergence of conflicted situations of civil and international strife, as well as gross injustices and mistreatment of groups and nations. Violence and injustice happen. The question is how such violence and injustice can be challenged and even transformed without resort to war. Just peacemaking is not so much a theory as a set of practices, and sometimes conditions, that contribute to the making of a just peace in such conflict situations.

Stassen has named and regularly repeated ten just peacemaking practices that he argues have proven themselves effective in accomplishing nonviolent conflict transformation. Under the category of "initiatives" he mentions nonviolent direct action, independent initiatives, cooperative conflict resolution, and acknowledgment of responsibility. These are all initiatives that any side in a situation of conflict, injustice, or war can take to change the dynamics of the situation. African-Americans could try nonviolent direct action to break the power of segregation but without taking up their own violent weapons. Superpower leaders could unilaterally announce weapons reductions and invite reciprocation during the Cold War. Either of the battling parties in late-stage apartheid South Africa could initiate just peacemaking talks. Germany's postwar prime minister could acknowledge responsibility for his nation's crimes against Poland during World War II, seeking forgiveness and reconciliation between the two nations. Of course, such initiatives were successfully taken in all of these cases.

Under the category of justice Stassen names two just peacemaking practices. These are advancing democracy and human rights, and fostering just and sustainable economic development. Resentments fester in or between nations when people's basic human rights are being violated, when some or all do not have (equal) access to participatory democratic processes, or when some or all do not have adequate or remotely equitable access to economic goods needed for life. These two just peacemaking practices push internal or external participants in conflict toward advancing justice in these areas and thus going to the root of civil or international conflicts. One thinks of the unjust situation facing Palestinians under military rule in large parts of the West Bank, as described just a bit in Sami Awad's essay, and of how desperately economic and political justice initiatives are needed there.

Under the category of love, Stassen names four other just peacemaking practices. Working with emerging cooperative forces in the international system primarily means leveraging and strengthening the connections that bind nations together and make war a really stupid choice. For example, the U.S. and China are so tightly bound together economically that war between today's two most powerful nations seems pretty much unthinkable, as it would crash at least their own two economies. Strengthening the United Nations and international efforts for cooperation and human rights can sound like dreamy idealist multilateralism. And it is true that Stassen is very much the multilateralist rather than unilateralist or American exceptionalist. But a more generous reading of this practice is simply that the stronger are the transnational connections, processes, and trusted adjudicatory conflict resolution mechanisms, the more likely are conflicts to be resolved short of war. Reducing offensive weapons and the weapons trade means more than just the truism that the global flow of small and large arms kills people. It also attends especially to the dangers of situations in which one side to a conflict has a disproportionate share of (especially, offensive) weapons and thus a temptation to use them in quest of a winning blow against their enemy. This issue became quite acute during various stages of the Cold War in terms of offensive nuclear weapons. Encouraging grassroots peacemaking groups and voluntary associations, the tenth just peacemaking practice, can be viewed at several levels. Internal to a nation, grassroots peacemakers can be truth-seeking and war-resisting resistance communities, acting as a brake on militarist or expansionist ambitions and calling their own people to a higher way. Grassroots peacemakers also sometimes develop internal communal practices of peacemaking, forgiveness, and conflict resolution that can model peacemaking to the broader society, or implement peacemaking nationally or internationally. They become the seeds of a newly peaceable society and international order; or at least, they have that potential.

Glen Stassen is both an empiricist and a devotee of scripture, especially the life and teachings of Jesus. Almost invariably when he presents just peacemaking he claims that it is both *effective* and *faithful to the way of Jesus—who is the ultimate "realist" because he is Creator and Lord of all.* Stassen is also attentive to psychological dynamics, such as empowerment and disempowerment. In his essay he claims that the just war versus pacifism debate is disempowering, but that just peacemaking practices are empowering, both intellectually and in actually making peace in a large number of conflicted and unjust situations that he can name. In grappling with Stassen's work it helps to know such background facts as that his father fought bravely in World War II and came back a committed multilateralist and peacemaker who helped found the United Nations; that Glen Stassen was trained in nuclear physics and for a time prepared for service in the nuclear weapons business; that he marched and organized during the civil rights movement and during the nuclear freeze campaign; and that he is of German background and a serious student of twentieth century and German history.

Stassen is also a patriot who loves the United States. But, like me, he believes that U.S. foreign and military policy since World War II has in many ways jumped the rails. He joins two of the other three writers we are considering in this section by offering intense criticism of post-9/11 U.S. government actions and also our ongoing government spending priorities. This may be one of the great cleavages in contemporary U.S. Christian thinking about peace and war; that is, deeply conflicted overall readings of the moral health and public policies of the United States itself. This split in how to "read" the U.S. deeply affects U.S. Christian ethical writings about peace and war.

Stassen regularly acknowledges but does not always emphasize that just peacemaking does not end the significance of the long argument between pacifists and just warriors. Just peacemaking does turn the question around in a most constructive way, however, teaching us to ask not "Is it ever permissible to go to war?" but instead "How do we make peace in this particular situation?" This movement from abstract moral rule debates to concrete moral practice implementation is indeed empowering. It would be helpful if Stassen here had acknowledged that just peacemaking practices themselves do not always work, in part because there are at least occasions in which bloodlust or aggrievement or greed render one or both parties to a conflict totally uninterested, at least for a time, in a just peace.

Stassen emphasizes that even our enemies have legitimate interests and that almost anyone can be invited into a thoughtful conversation about their own legitimate interests. Stassen has emphasized that North Korea and Iran, for example, have security interests that can be engaged. It is good to be reminded that not every adversary is a Black Knight who can only be stopped by cutting off his arms and legs. Not every leader is Hitler, and not every negotiation is the shameful appeasement reached in 1938 Munich. But Stassen would help his own cause if at times he said more about those moments when the leader is like Hitler and a negotiated peace would be like Munich.

Looking back at all four of the presentations reviewed in this first section, it is striking that the activities of the state rather than the church receive primary attention. My essay briefly acknowledges a difference in roles and responsibilities between church and state. Patterson emphasizes just war theory as a grand tradition of the church. Stassen speaks about creating peace churches and grassroots peacemaker groups in churches. But overall, I am reminded that the old Christian arguments about "the ethics of war" generally direct Christian attention away from the church and toward the state. This is because it is states that make war. Pacifism says either states should not make war or Christians can't participate in a state's war. Just war theory says states sometimes can and should make war and Christians should participate in just wars. Even just peacemaking generally emphasizes that states make war but should adopt other practices that prevent many of these wars from being made. The church becomes a community pressing for that kind of state peacemaking and resisting reckless war-making states. (Though sometimes church groups themselves become just peacemakers. Stassen's essay is a bridge to the others.)

Evangelical Peacemaking in Practice

It is fascinating to notice that the state is generally not the focus of any of the other eleven essays in this collection. None of the other authors are trying to offer a Christian ethic of war. Mainly coming out of congregations and parachurch organizations, the remaining authors focus almost all of their attention on Christian peacemaking as an expression of gospel witness, service, and love. The essays are not about what states should and shouldn't do or how Christians should posture themselves in relation to states. Instead they are about what congregations, parachurch organizations, and individual Christians are already doing to bear peaceable Christian witness and participate in making peace. In the concluding section of this essay, I will highlight key themes in these eleven essays.

NGO Peacemaking: Creative Diplomacy and Ground-Level Peacemaking

Geoff Tunnicliffe's World Evangelical Alliance is a 160-year-old organization that has primarily been known for missions work and fostering theological discussion internal to the global evangelical community. I had no occasion to encounter it until recently. But clearly Tunnicliffe has sought to move the organization toward a justice and peacemaking focus, while also appropriately positioning the WEA as a third, co-equal player in a global ecumenical scene that heretofore primarily has involved the World Council of Churches and the Roman Catholic Church.

This posture shift on the part of WEA reflects the growing clout of the burgeoning evangelical community worldwide, while also signals its efforts to mobilize that clout for service to a war-torn and deeply unjust world. Evangelicals have long been known for evangelism and missions, with missions often including relief and development work as well as other works of service and mercy noted by Tunnicliffe in his article. As he points out with reference to Sri Lanka, part of Christianity's contribution in ethnically divided societies is simply to *be the church*, that is, to create ethnically inclusive congregations centered on the reconciling love of Jesus Christ. This is the work of classic evangelism and missions, and it is a theme central to the New Testament witness (cf. Eph 2:11–22). But Tunnicliffe and his movement are also doing a variety of justice- and peacemaking initiatives on the ground, and increasingly Tunnicliffe himself is getting involved in direct diplomacy as a representative leader of global evangelical Christianity. It is fascinating to contemplate a future for evangelical Christian leaders as global diplomats (a role long played by Catholic popes), and to see the gradual institutionalization of a vision for Christian engagement that includes grassroots peacemaking and conflict resolution. These are very encouraging developments.

The Fellowship of Reconciliation was founded one hundred years ago out of evangelical Christianity and on the brink of the great slaughter now known as World War I. Its identity gradually broadened from evangelical to ecumenical and then from ecumenical to interfaith, and the activities Mark Johnson describes appear to be primarily "civilian diplomacy" and some quite bold grassroots peacemaking. Johnson claims that FOR remains a "profoundly evangelical movement," but I am quite confident that its trajectory from evangelical to ecumenical to interfaith is *not* what most evangelicals are hoping will happen with their own organizations today. Indeed, Tunnicliffe of WEA notes his involvement as a leader in "Religions for Peace," an interfaith effort, and immediately acknowledges that "some in our community may question this kind of interaction, [but] we must recognize that we have a strong biblical mandate to promote peace building and join others in building more harmonious societies." Evangelical Christianity is particularistically Christian, and its history includes a great commitment to preserving the integrity of (some version of orthodox Protestant) Christian doctrine. Tunnicliffe implicitly seeks to fight off the worry that WEA's ecumenical and interfaith engagements will eventually lead it to become an interfaith social justice movement like, well, FOR.

This kind of worry—or responding to this kind of worry—haunts a number of these essays. My own view is that the world needs both religiously thick, particular, devoutly evangelical Christian movements and communities, and it needs members from precisely such communities to engage the broader world of ideas, religions, and the human suffering caused by war. There is room at the peacemaking table for organizations operating from very different religious models.

Jim Wallis founded and leads a much younger NGO, Sojourners, based in Washington. His essay was partly crafted in response to my pessimistic statement in the first chapter about how little influence Christians seem to have today on U.S. foreign policy. His review of almost fifty years of ecumenical and not just evangelical foreign policy engagement was a good rejoinder. A close reading of the cases he mentions illustrates a wide variety of ways that Christians have worked for less killing and more justice in U.S. foreign policy, as well as times Christians have surprised everyone with gracious initiatives toward, for example, Muslims who are being mistreated or derided right here in America. Especially notable to me are the little-known examples of Christians placing themselves right in the middle of conflict zones, in Latin America and elsewhere, with the hope of deterring the U.S. or its allies from bombing or attacking those communities. Such strategies are also mentioned in Mark Johnson's essay. That is courageous Christian peacemaking—taking risk upon one's own head, standing in solidarity with threatened people, and in the absence of an ability to reason with policymakers or military leaders, simply to place oneself between the bombs and guns and their intended victims. That's a very Jesus-like kind of thing to do, and it inspires admiration, even awe.

Rick Love is the founder and leader of the newest evangelical NGO engaged with peace issues. A former missionary of impeccable evangelical credentials and deep experience in the Muslim world, Love now feels called to this work with Peace Catalyst International. He says: "We are pioneering what it means to be evangelical peacemakers. We are truly peacemakers and we are truly evangelical. We share the gospel of peace and we pursue the peace of God." His organization is new but his vision is big. He sketches it in terms of six levels of peacemaking, ranging from inner personal peace to international peace. Only God knows what his organization will ultimately do, but this initiative is yet another exciting sign of a broadening and deepening of an evangelical peace witness—and peacemaking practice.

Deep Christian Engagement with Muslims and Islam

Joseph Cumming, Douglas Johnston, and David Shenk are among those in our collection who write of increasingly intense and constructive Christian engagement with Muslims and Islam. While some Christians responded to 9/11 with blanket condemnations of Islam—mainly based on very little information and no personal relationships—Cumming, Johnston, Shenk and others instead engaged in increasingly profound relationship-building within the Muslim world and with the American Muslim community. These efforts have constructive implications for U.S. foreign policy, if our government will pay attention.

Joseph Cumming's narrative speaks to the value of cultivating personal relationships with media, political, and religious leaders in the global Muslim community. His capacity to communicate successfully with Al Jazeera during the flap over the "Innocence of Muslims" "movie" was critically important. His dialogues with Sheikh Fadlallah in Beirut reveal the value of knowing Muslim tradition from the inside and being able to explain Christian convictions in ways that draw meaningful connections to Islam. How many Christians could have managed conversations like the ones reported in his chapter?

Douglas Johnston's essay makes the practical point that the best antidote to extremist ideology is better ideology, a point that is certainly true of extremist religion over against more tolerant religion. His essay is a reminder that it is foolish to speak of any religion univocally, as in "Christianity/Islam/Judaism is a religion of ___ (peace, violence, love, hate, etc.)." The oldest world religions are like continents. They require exploration, and intrepid explorers discover both beauties and terrors in each world religion. A key role of leaders within religious communities is to tame the terrors and advance the beauties of their faiths and their traditions, in part by deepening the practice and articulation of the best traditions of each faith, as David Shenk tries to do with the peacemaking strands within Christianity. Yet Johnston shows that skillful intervention by trusted outside voices sometimes can help religious insiders with their own internal religion-shaping processes. Thus it comes as very happy news that ICRJ has been able to gain access to Pakistani madrasas to affect the kind of religious instruction there. This kind of engagement with global Islam strikes me as hugely important. Meanwhile, ICRJ's engagement with the American Muslim community is strategic in many ways, notably in advancing U.S. civic peace and security and also bearing witness globally to ways Muslims can be faithful in Islamic practice even in very pluralistic contemporary Western societies.

"The Insanity of Grace"

The title for this final section comes from Lisa Gibson's riveting account of her journey toward forgiving and serving the Libyan people after the Libyan government murdered her own brother and hundreds of others over Lockerbie in 1988.

"The insanity of grace" is an apt description for Gibson's response to her brother's cruel murder. It is unimaginable that a person who did not share Gibson's demanding and personally transformative kind of religious faith could reason his or her way to the radical service and forgiveness that she mustered in the name of Christ. Certainly an emphasis merely on justice would not have done it. Nor would an emphasis on national pride. Nor, for that matter, would a just war emphasis on self-defense and legitimate retribution. This is *grace* that we see in Gibson's story.

And there is indeed a certain "insanity" about it. There is nothing rational about writing a letter to the murderer of your brother, or bringing a gift to Muammar Gaddafi while offering him a forgiveness that he did not seek.

Nor is there anything especially sane about Palestinian Christian Sami Awad building a relationship with the Israeli captain who routinely orders his beatings during protests. Or about his effort to focus not on the unjust Israeli Occupation of Palestine but on the spiritual-moral "occupation" of peacemaking and recognition of the dignity of all parties to that terribly conflicted situation. Or about him naming the real spiritual struggle as not between Israelis and Palestinians but between those willing to recognize the dignity of the other side and those unwilling to do so, a line that runs through the heart of both communities.

Nor is there anything remotely normal about Mennonite leader Shenk's forays engaging Muslims, in some cases radical Muslims, in Kosovo, Egypt, Indonesia, and Iran. Do not let this collection go back on your virtual or real bookshelf without rereading his account of sitting in dialogue with the well-armed brothers of Hizbullah in Indonesia.

I said near the beginning of this chapter that "evangelicalism's passion and zeal tends to make its religiosity serve as a kind of *accelerant*, for good or ill; thus it is important for evangelical leaders to direct this religion's energies in the most constructive ways possible." That is the extraordinary power of real, vital, living religions, which govern believers' lives and direct their behavior toward what they believe God wants them to do—not what is merely rational or preferential on their own part. This extraordinary power can yield men hijacking airplanes and suicidally running them into office buildings, or it can yield grieving sisters and courageous Mennonites and former governors and bruised Palestinians going to Libya, Yemen, Afghanistan, Indonesia, Iran, Pakistan, Egypt, and Jerusalem loving people and making peace *because that's just what Christ-followers do.*

The same serious faith also might just yield Texas megachurch pastors like Bob Roberts taking large numbers of politically and theologically conservative Christians to Hanoi—the ultimate enemy city of another generation—and to Afghanistan. And it might lead him to care about the religious liberty rights not just of his co-religionists in Muslim lands but also Muslims in our land. Pastors in certain kinds of churches are understood by the people who pay their salaries to be employed to listen to the radical things God calls Christ-followers to do, to demand such activities from their congregants, and then to facilitate opportunities for them to go out and do those things. In these kinds of churches, when the radical things God leads such pastors to tell their people to do seem especially insane, abnormal, and un-American, then that's precisely when the people know that God has really spoken to their pastor. That kind of religious ecology in a church is both unusual and exceedingly fertile. It creates religious worlds in which people go out and do bold things, because their God is real, and alive, and demanding, and empowering. And because their Savior Jesus loved humanity to the point of dying on a cruel Roman cross, and told them to love everyone, especially their enemies.

Evangelical Peacemakers

There is evidence in this collection of sophisticated Christian theorizing about the ethics of war and peace, all striving for a just and peaceful world. These are evangelical peacemakers.

There is evidence of increasingly sophisticated Christian NGOs and their leaders engaging both the U.S. government and global conflict situations with skillful initiatives and interventions. These are evangelical peacemakers.

There is evidence of deep Christian penetration into the Muslim world, and into the American Muslim community, for the purposes of a new kind of Christian mission of international peacemaking and facilitation of moderate, tolerant, morally constructive leaders and versions of Islam (and also Christianity). These are evangelical peacemakers.

And then there is evidence of "the insanity of grace"—the transformative power of Jesus Christ as he continues to forge lives of courage, mercy, and love in our war-torn world. Evangelical peacemakers, indeed!

Bibliography

Allen, Bob. "Colleges, universities, pledge to interfaith community service." *Word & Way*. Online: http://www.wordandway.org/index.php?option=com_content&task=view&id=2042&Itemid=53.

Appleby, Scott. *The Ambivalence of the Sacred*. Lanham, MD: Rowman & Littlefield, 1999.

Aquinas, Thomas. *Summa Theologica*. Translated by Fathers of the English Dominican Province. New York: Christian Classics, 1981.

Bacevich, Andrew J. *Washington Rules: America's Path to Permanent War*. New York: Holt, 2010.

Bell, Daniel M., Jr. *Just War as Christian Discipleship*. Grand Rapids: Brazos, 2009.

Biggar, Nigel. *Burying the Past: Making Peace and Doing Justice after Civil Conflict*. Washington, DC: Georgetown University Press, 2003.

Brzezinski, Zbigniew. *Strategic Vision*. New York: Basic, 2012.

Charles, J. Darryl, and Timothy Demy. *War, Peace, and Christianity: Questions and Answers from a Just War Perspective*. New York: Crossway, 2010.

"A Common Word Between Us and You." Online: http://www.acommonword.com/the-acw-document.

Elshtain, Jean Bethke. *Just War Against Terror*. New York: Basic, 2003.

Epp, Roger. "The Augustinian Moment in International Politics." *International Politics Research Papers*, No. 10. Aberystwyth, UK: Department of International Politics, University College of Wales, 1991.

Follman, Mark, et al. "U.S. Mass Shootings, 1982–2012: Data From Mother Jones' Investigation." Online: http://www.motherjones.com/politics/2012/12/mass-shootings-mother-jones-full-data.

Griffith, Lee. *The War on Terrorism and the Terror of God*. Grand Rapids: Eerdmans, 2002.

Griswold, Eliza. *The Tenth Parallel: Dispatches from the Fault Line between Islam and Christianity*. New York: Farrar, Straus, and Giroux, 2010.

Gushee, David P. *The Sacredness of Human Life*. Grand Rapids: Eerdmans, 2013.

Harper, Lisa Sharon, and D. C. Innes. *Left, Right, and Christ: Evangelical Faith in Politics*. Boise, ID: Russell Media, 2011.

Interfaith Works. "History and Mission." Online: http://www.iworksmc.org/a-history-mission.html.

Interfaith Youth Core. "About IFYC." Online: http://www.ifyc.org/about-us.

Johnson, James Turner. *The Just War Tradition and the Restraint of War*. Princeton, NJ: Princeton University Press, 1981.

———. *Morality and Contemporary Warfare*. New Haven, CT: Yale University Press, 1999.

Kaplan, Robert D. "The Statesman: In Defense of Henry Kissinger." *The Atlantic* (May 2013) 71–78.

Kateregga, Badu D., and David W. Shenk. *A Muslim and a Christian in Dialogue.* Harrisonburg, VA: Herald, 2011.

Kristof, Nicholas. "War Wounds." Online: http://www.nytimes.com/2012/08/12/opinion/sunday/war-wounds.html?pagewanted=all.

Lampman, Jane. "Muslim reformer's 'heresy': The Islamic state is a dead end." *Christian Science Monitor*, April 2, 2008. Online: http://www.csmonitor.com/USA/2008/0402/p01s01–usgn.html.

Leiken, Robert S., and Steven Brooke. "The Moderate Muslim Brotherhood." *Foreign Affairs*, 86:2 (2007) 107–21.

Letter of the Most Rev. Dr. Mouneer Hanna Anis, Bishop of the Episcopal /Anglican Diocese of Egypt with North Africa and the Horn of Africa, President Bishop of the Episcopal/Anglican Province of Jerusalem and the Middle East, to David Shenk. August 5, 2012.

Lewis, C. S. *Mere Christianity.* New York: Simon and Schuster, 1996.

———. "Why I Am Not A Pacifist." In *The Weight of Glory and Other Addresses,* 64–90. New York: Collier, 1980.

"List of Countries by Military Expenditure." Online: http://en.wikipedia.org/wiki/List_of_countries_by_military_expenditures.

Luce, Jim. "Muslims & Non-Muslims Hear about Terrorist Threat, Solutions at Harvard Club." *HuffPost World*, June 29, 2010. Online: http://www.huffingtonpost.com/jim-luce/muslim-non-muslims-hear-a_b_629437.html.

O'Donovan, Oliver. *The Just War Revisited.* Cambridge: Cambridge University Press, 2003.

Orend, Brian. "Justice After War." *Ethics and International Affairs* 16:1 (Spring 2002) 43–56.

———. *The Morality of War.* Peterborough, ON: Broadview, 2006.

Pape, Robert A. *Dying to Win: The Strategic Logic of Suicide Terrorism.* New York: Random House, 2005.

Patterson, Eric. *Just War Thinking: Pragmatism and Morality in the Struggle Against Contemporary Threat.* Lanham, MD: Lexington, 2007.

———. *Ending Wars Well: Order, Justice, and Conciliation in Post-Conflict.* New Haven, CT: Yale University Press, 2012.

———. *Politics in a Religious World.* New York: Continuum, 2011.

Patterson, Eric, ed. *The Christian Realists.* Lanham, MD: University of America Press, 2003.

———. *Ethics beyond War's End.* Washington, DC: Georgetown University Press, 2012.

Pearson Higher Education. "Religion." *Universalizing Religions.* Online: www.pearsonhighered.com/samplechapter/013243573x.pdf.

Peck, M. Scott. Online: http://www.brainyquote.com/quotes/quotes/m/mscottpec160100.html.

Pew Forum on Religion and Public Life. "Tolerance and Tension, Islam and Christianity in Sub-Saharan Africa." The Pew Research Center, April 15, 2010. Online: http://www.pewforum.org/executive-summary-islam-and-christianity-in-sub-saharan-africa.aspx.

Philpott, Daniel, et al. *God's Century.* New York: Norton, 2011.

Philpott, Daniel. *Just and Unjust Peace: An Ethic of Political Reconciliation*. New York: Oxford University Press, 2012.

Ramsey, Paul. *Basic Christian Ethics*. Louisville: Westminster John Knox, 1950.

Russell, Frederick H. *The Just War in the Middle Ages*. Cambridge: Cambridge University Press, 1975.

Shenk, David W. "The Gospel of Reconciliation within the Wrath of Nations." *International Bulletin of Missionary Research* 32:1 (2008) 3–9.

Staberock, Gerald. Interview with Lisa Sharon Harper. February 3, 2011.

Stassen, Glen H. *The Journey into Peacemaking*. Memphis: Brotherhood Commission of the SBC, 1983.

———. *Just Peacemaking: Transforming Initiatives for Justice and Peace*. Louisville: Westminster John Knox: 1992.

———. *A Thicker Jesus: Incarnational Discipleship in a Secular Age*. Louisville: Westminster John Knox: 2012.

Stassen, Glen H., ed. *Formation for Just Peacemaking*. Eugene, OR: Wipf and Stock, 2012

———. *Just Peacemaking*. Cleveland: Pilgrim Press, 2008.

———. *Just Peacemaking: The New Paradigm for the Ethics of Peace and War*. Cleveland: Pilgrim, 2004/2008.

———. *Just Peacemaking: Ten Practices for Abolishing War*. Cleveland: Pilgrim Press, 1998.

Stephenson, William R., Jr. *Christian Love and Just War: Moral Paradox and Political Life in St. Augustine and His Modern Interpreters*. Macon, GA: Mercer University Press, 1987.

Stiglitz, Joseph. *The Price of Inequality*. New York: Norton, 2012.

Stockman, David E. "Paul Ryan's Fairy-Tale Budget Plan." Online: http://www.nytimes.com/2012/08/14/opinion/paul-ryans-fairy-tale-budget-plan.html?_r=1.

Tappert, Theodore G., ed. *Selected Writings of Martin Luther, 1529–1546*. Minneapolis: Fortress, 1966.

Thistlethwaite, Susan Brooks, ed. *Interfaith Just Peacemaking: Jewish, Christian, and Muslim Perspectives on the New Paradigm of Peace and War*. New York: Palgrave–MacMillan: 2012.

Walzer, Michael. *Just and Unjust Wars*. 3rd ed. New York: Basic, 2000.

Weigel, George. *Tranquillitas Ordinis: The Present Failure and Future Promise of American Catholic Thought on War and Peace*. Oxford: Oxford University Press, 1987.

The White House. "The President's Interfaith and Community Service Campus Challenge." Online: http://www.whitehouse.gov/administration/eop/ofbnp/interfaithservice.

"William Hague: UN has failed on Syria." *BBC News*, March 12, 2011. Online: http://www.bbc.co.uk/news/world–middle-east-17339013.

World Evangelical Alliance. "Peace and Reconcilation." Online: http://www.weapri.org/about-2.